# Acknowledgements

This book is dedicated to my mother Irena Ogonowska and my aunt Teresa Ogonowska. They are the survivors, and I wish to thank them for their love and support in the writing of this book.

I would like to acknowledge the following people for their help in many different ways. Pieter Watson for his unqualified support; Allie Webber whose friendship has inspired me to persevere; Bozennia, Henryk and Baska Wiek, Jozef and Marie Kubiak, Helena Wypych, Irena and Polek Kilczewski, Leon and Jadwiga Domanski, Stefa and Jozef Zawada, Piotr Przychodko, Wanda Ellis, Wisia Schwieters, Dr John and Halina Kania, Mietek and Danuta Murawaski, Krystyna Downie and all the Poles who allowed me to talk with them about their past lives; my father Ken Coates for his keen interest; Jane Parkin for her insights and encouragement. A Queen Elizabeth II Arts Council major project grant helped make the writing of this book possible.

# Krystyna's Story

## A Polish refugee's journey

Halina Ogonowska-Coates

Longacre Press

# Na Pamięć

*Na wieczna pamięć wszystkich naszych*
*Polakow ojcow matek i dzieci ktorzy zginęli*
*w czasie drugiej wojny swiatowei*

First published in 1992 by Bridget Williams Books Ltd
Second edition published in 1998 by Shoal Bay Press Ltd

This edition published by Longacre Press, 2008
30 Moray Place, Dunedin, New Zealand

Copyright © Halina Ogonowska-Coates 1992, 1998, 2008

ISBN 978 1877460 166

A catalogue record for this book is available from
the National Library of New Zealand.

Design: Katy Yiakmis
Printed by Griffin Press, Australia

www.longacre.co.nz

# The First Journey

This could be my mother's story. It could belong to any one of the two million Poles who were deported to the Soviet Union during the Second World War. But in a way it is nobody's story, for who can remember all that happened after the soldiers came and took them away?

As a child I loved my mother but she seemed different from other mothers. She didn't know how old she was. She couldn't remember where she was born. I wondered what had happened to her that she could have forgotten such important things. It had something to do with the Second World War.

When I grew older I wanted to get to know my mother and to find out about her past. Eventually I learned that she was among the seven hundred and thirty-two Polish children who had survived forced deportation to the Soviet Union and had travelled half way across the world to take refuge in New Zealand in 1944. My mother was reluctant to talk about her past. She said it was too sad, but I kept asking her questions. I wanted to know what had happened to my Polish grandmother. I wanted to know about the place where my mother was born. Slowly my mother began to talk to me. We sat together for hours, talking and crying, putting together the tattered fragments that were her memories, but there were many missing pieces. My mother had been a small child when she was taken from her Polish home.

I went to visit her Polish friends to find out more. These people had endured similar harrowing experiences, but they took me into their hearts as my mother's daughter and told me stories that will always haunt the corners of my mind.

Slowly my mother's childhood came alive to me. I can close my eyes and see her playing in the fields outside Baranowiczie, a small girl with blue eyes and blonde hair. This could be her story.

## Chapter 1

I was born in Poland, beautiful Poland. I can remember so clearly the house where I was born, the wide front verandah and the huge windows looking out on to the fields, and the forest beyond. My childhood was short but there are little pockets of memory that remain so clearly. I remember my mother. Her face is etched firmly in my mind. I can see her lying there in the big four-poster bed, her blue eyes shining out from the starched pillows. I wish that she could smile to me now.

It was a happy childhood. I remember learning to walk in the warmth of the big kitchen, clinging to my mother's skirts as she worked. The smell of *pierogi* and *barszcz* was thick and heavy in the air. Mama was always stirring and tasting, or bending to look into the hot oven. I loved to stand at the big scrubbed wooden table beside my sister

Marysia as she kneaded the dough for bread, sliced cabbages for sauerkraut and threaded onions ready to hang under the verandah roof to dry.

We were a farming family living just outside the town of Baranowiczie. The land was our livelihood and our wooden house sat solid and low among the fields like a *babchia* with her skirts spread. Behind the house were the stables, the woodshed, the pigsty and a byre for the cows. I loved to play in the orchard, climbing the apple trees or just lying in the shade listening to the birds and whispering the names of the people in my family, Mama, Marysia, Feliks and Tata, whispering them over and over like a magic incantation. I loved Mama but Tata was my hero. I knew every curve of his face underneath that bushy beard which tickled my nose whenever he kissed me. Every evening I waited by the stables for Tata to come in from the fields. I was so eager to see him, impatient to feel those strong arms throw me up, flying high in the air, one … two … three … four times until Mama called to him to put me down.

Winter was my favourite time of the year. Outside it snowed and snowed, soft white layers that piled huge blankets on the ground, up to the windows and then higher until all you could see was the roof of our house. Inside, the fire was glowing night and day. Tata dug a corridor through the snow to get to the road. I remember standing just outside the door, bundled up in shawls and watching him digging and throwing the shovelfuls of snow up over his shoulder and on to the pile above him. Our house seemed so warm and safe. I knew that no matter how much snow fell we would be protected from the cold weather. During the long winter afternoons Mama and Marysia took up their embroidery and sat by the stove. I sat on the floor beside them, running the brightly coloured embroidery threads through my fingers and making bright patterns on the floor. Mama and Marysia talked softly as they bent their heads over the white linen. Their hands seemed to work in unison as they picked out the tiny stitches. Mama smiled at my tangle of threads on the floor. She put down her needle and tugged at my plaits.

'Come and sit beside me, Kryska,' she said. 'Watch carefully and I will teach you how to sew.'

But I was too young and impatient. I didn't like using the sharp needle that pricked my thumbs and made long ragged stitches which were so unlike the neat tidy rows that Mama and Marysia made. Marysia tried to guide my hand but I still couldn't do it. I just wanted to sit there in the warm glow of the stove playing imaginary games.

The days and weeks of our lives had a simple regularity.

Things changed slowly with the movement of the seasons. We watched for the storks in spring and helped with the harvest in autumn. Years were marked with name days, weddings and feast days. I felt the ebb and flow of life and knew my place within it.

Then suddenly everything changed. It happened without warning and dragged us along with it. I remember the date. September the first, 1939.

Poland was attacked on two sides. From the west came

the Germans with troops, tanks and squadrons of bombers. From the east came the Soviets, marching into Poland with men and guns. It was as if hell had broken open. The earth shook under the pounding of German guns and shivered with the rumble of advancing tanks. In the skies the birds fled and the sun was obscured with German planes which bombed the factories, roads, bridges, fuel stores and the army headquarters. Poland was betrayed. Under the terms of the Ribbentrop-Molotov Pact signed in August 1939, the Soviet Union and Germany divided Poland. The German Reich annexed 73,000 miles of Polish territory and 22 million people. The Soviets took 78,000 square miles and 13 million people.

I was eight years old. I have no photographs or documents but I can remember what I saw. These things are so deeply embedded in my mind that they cannot be erased. I can feel the fear rising. I cannot hear anything above the noise of the planes buzzing over my head. Little fast planes. You could hear them before you could see them. It was an urgent angry noise. There were big open fields in front of our house and the planes came right down low, dropping leaflets and sweets on to the fields. As soon as the planes disappeared my brother Feliks rushed outside and started picking up the sweets.

'Idiot!' Mama shouted. 'Come back here.' Feliks ran to her, leaping over the furrows with his hands full of paper and pretty-coloured sweets. Mama grabbed his shoulders and pushed him back down the steps away from the house. 'Throw them away,' she screamed. Her voice was quavery and shaking. 'Throw them down and come inside to wash.' Feliks dropped his sweets into the pig pen. Our huge sow and her piglets gobbled them up.

'Feliks!' Mama called. He went inside reluctantly. No one enjoyed a wash under Mama's supervision. She was so strict about scrubbing every corner of your body — behind the ears, the back of the neck, between the toes. And you had to work quickly. She heated only one panful for each person and the water didn't stay warm for very long. I stayed outside to watch the pigs. They ate the handful of sweets in one swallow but I could see that there were lots more lying out in the fields. I didn't know why Mama was so cross with Feliks for picking up the sweets that had fallen out of the sky, and ran to plead with her.

'Please Mama,' I begged. 'Can I have just one of those pretty sweets?'

Mama stopped pouring hot water into the basin and looked very grave. She crouched down beside me and put her arms around my shoulders. Her face was very close to mine. 'Krystyna,' she said, 'those sweets are poisoned.'

I didn't believe her but in the morning the pigs were dead. We forgot about the planes with the excitement of preparing for Christmas. Mama and Marysia cleaned and scrubbed the whole house. They aired the feather eiderdowns in the guest rooms, getting ready for visitors. All day and half the night pots were bubbling on the stove. The house was heavy with the smell of yeast and spices.

Feliks went with Tata to help cut down the tree. We had chosen it in summer, a small pine with pretty outstretched branches. It had to look beautiful from every angle but when they carried the tree into the house it was too tall to stand upright. Tata hauled it back outside, leaving a trail of pine needles on the floor. Marysia and I picked them up. The floor was so shiny you could see yourself reflected. I rubbed the pine needles between my hands and sniffed the smell. It mingled with the floor polish, a deep heady fragrance. In the evening we decorated the tree. Tata brought in the sheaves of wheat, offerings for a good harvest next year, and Marysia tied them together with gay red and white bows. They looked like sentinels standing in front of the dresser, guarding our home.

That night the whole house was still and silent, waiting for the *wi gilia*, the Polish Christmas Eve. I lay in my bed breathing the sweet scent of the tree and listening to Mama and Tata talking together. Life felt so safe and warm. I fell asleep curled tight in my bed, lying below the headboard that Dziadek had carved when I was born. 'Bless this child,' it read.

Things were changing. We had visitors every day. Mama was always opening the door to welcome men, women and children we had never seen before. They carried big bundles and looked as if they wore several layers of clothes. Mama invited them inside. They put their bundles in the guest room and sat at our table eating as if they had not seen food for a very long time. Feliks and I poked and pried while the strangers ate and talked to Mama in low worried voices. We peered into the bundles while no one was looking. I saw blankets, spoons, forks, books and photograph albums. Well wrapped in the corner of one haversack I could feel the hard edge of a candlestick. Feliks furtively undid the straps and rummaged inside.

'It's silver,' he said, 'and there are silver knives and spoons as well.'

We wondered why these visitors were carrying so much with them. They looked worried and tired. The children who travelled with them sat in the corner and slept.

'Mama,' I asked one night when she tucked me into my bed. 'Where do those people come from?'

She held me close and kissed my head. 'They are running away,' she said. 'You must be kind to them and do all that you can to help them.' 'What are they running away from?' I asked her, wriggling out of her hug. I traced the wrinkles of a frown on her forehead and was suddenly frightened. 'I don't know,' Mama said, sighing deeply. 'Now God bless you.'

She kissed me and quietly closed the door. I lay in bed but the chill had come closer. There was uneasiness in the air. I buried my head in my feather pillow and cried for the frightened worried people who visited our house. In the morning my tears faded. Life seemed to have the same regularity. Every morning Tata got up before dawn and went out into the fields. He worked all day with men to help him, ploughing, harrowing and sowing according to the seasons of the year. Mama rose at six and lit the stove. As soon as I smelt the coffee I would run to the kitchen in my nightdress, begging for a cup. I loved to sit at the table in the morning and drink coffee with Mama. She would talk about her dreams and ask about mine. I sat close against the softness of her side and talked about horses, fields of flowers and pretty dresses. Mama laughed and patted my head.

'Kryska,' she said, 'you are too young. We will have to wait until you grow up before your dreams have deep meanings.'

She finished her coffee and began to cook breakfast. The morning stillness of the kitchen was broken. My brother Feliks appeared, dressed in his dark blue cadet uniform. He gobbled his breakfast and left for the long ride to school as soon as he had eaten. And then Marysia was at my elbow, telling me to go and get dressed. Marysia had finished attending school and as soon as her boyfriend Andrej had finished his military service we were going to have a wedding. Marysia stayed at home and helped Mama with the work. She was an excellent cook. Her *sernik* was even better than Mama's.

Once I was dressed, the morning had ended. It was time to eat and hurry down the road to school. I always wanted to stay behind and work in the kitchen with Marysia and Mama.

'Please, please, let me stay at home,' I would beg, drying the dishes so fast they were in danger of slipping through my fingers and crashing to the floor. I always hoped that Mama would give in but she usually lost her patience and pushed me out the door.

'Off you go,' she'd say, giving me a quick kiss on the fore-head. 'If you don't go to school you will always be a simpleton.'

One morning Tata was not outside when I got up. He sat in his study with the door shut, listening to the radio. When I got home from school he was still in there. Mama and Marysia were in the kitchen making brawn. There was no singing and laughing, no jokes about weddings and marriages. Mama was worried and silent. She frowned when Marysia suggested that we take a picnic to the river. 'Keep the child quiet,' was all she said and she went into Tata's study and shut the door.

I envied them sitting there together, surrounded by books and ledgers steeped with the leathery scent of Tata's pipe. I loved our house. The deep glow of the polished wood floors, the intricate flowery patterns embroidered on the thick linen curtains, and the drawing room with its rich red carpet and silver-framed photographs of Mama and Tata's wedding day. It was not a large estate but there was enough for us to live comfortably and to pay the men who helped Tata in the fields.

In the evening when we were all sitting around the kitchen table, Tata told us that he had received his army papers. He was an officer on reserve and was called up because the Polish army was mobilised for action.

'Children,' he said, 'I am going away to fight for Poland. Feliks, you must look after your mother and your sisters. You must all stay together, whatever happens.' And we knelt around the table and prayed for Poland and for Tata. After dinner Tata went out into the fields to plant seed for the new season. He worked all night, walking up and down the furrows with the seed bag on his back.

Mama sat silently at the table. Then she took Tata's uniform from the chest in their bedroom. She pressed the shirts, even though they were already clean and stiffly starched. I polished Tata's boots and Feliks worked his saddle until it was so shiny I was afraid that Tata would slip off when he mounted. Marysia packed Tata's saddlebags with the things he would need — food, soap, candles, towels, a small picture of Mama, and underwear which she wrapped around his revolver.

I went to the stables at dawn to feed Tata's horse, stuffing him with oats until his girth was straining.

'Enough,' Tata said. He was standing behind me. His face was dirty and tired but he scooped me up in his arms, tickling my face with his beard. 'If you feed this horse any more he will burst.'

I pressed my face into his neck, smelling his strong man smell, and then he was gone. He changed into his uniform and led his horse from the stable. We stood outside while he kissed each of us, holding our Mama, our brave mother, in a tight embrace. We waved as he rode away, still standing in a line in front of the house with tears running down our faces. I knew that he would be back soon, riding home for Mama's name day. I couldn't wait to see my father again.

It was quiet without Tata. Nothing was the same. No one came to work in the fields. After school Feliks milked the cows, fed the horses and tried to keep up with the work in the fields. Mama and Marysia were busy all day in the kitchen, baking loaf after loaf of bread. Usually they made bread twice a week but now they baked every day. The smell filled the house, but somehow it was not as cheering as usual, and after they had baked the loaves Mama dried them on top of the oven. Bread was so delicious fresh, I couldn't understand why Mama wanted to dry it out.

'What are you doing to the bread, Mama?' I asked. 'Sssshhh …' Marysia said, running her hands through my hair. 'Don't trouble Mama with questions.'

When the loaves of bread were hard and dry Mama stored them in sacks. It seemed such a strange thing to do that I thought maybe Mama was going mad and Marysia didn't want to tell me.

Nighttime changed. We went to sleep as usual, but during the night Marysia woke me and hustled me out of bed. My clothes were always ready in a heap on the floor. It didn't matter what you wore, Mama never noticed if I had mismatched socks or the hem of my dress was torn. My legs felt heavy as I walked to the kitchen where Mama was standing with her coat on, making coffee. Her hair was loose, rippling in thick curly waves down her back. Mama never wore her hair down during the day. It was always plaited and pinned in a roll at the back of her head.

We stumbled outside in the dark and lay flat in the furrows or perched in the orchard's trees like strange, outsized birds. The worst hiding place was the hen house. It was so crowded in there as we crouched among the hens which made little shuffling noises around us.

'What are we hiding from?' I asked Mama one night as we lay with our faces pressed into the cold earth.

'The Russians,' Mama muttered, turning her head sideways.

'But why?' Feliks asked.

'Because they are taking people away.'

In the half light of morning I could see that she was crying. I had so many questions but I kept my mouth shut and my lips tightly sealed. I wanted to be as brave as the rest of my family. Now I needed to be an adult, too.

We walked home in the dawn, stiff with fatigue and the pain of standing up all night. Feliks ran on ahead. He liked to get home first to light the stove and make the coffee. Strong hot coffee that gave us hope. I trailed through the fields behind Marysia, following her step for step. A little pattern formed in my tired mind and I hummed it to the tune of my favourite song. Marysia turned around and smiled. I loved her so much. We joined hands and tramped together through the fields, singing and swinging our hands high in the air. Even Mama began to sing along. Then we heard the screaming.

'It's Feliks,' Marysia cried, and she began to run. Mama went with her, leaping over the furrows, shouting and calling Feliks's name.

I crouched there alone, holding my hands over my ears, trying to block out the noise of Feliks screaming. I huddled there until I felt someone shaking me.

'Come, Krystyna,' Marysia said gently, putting her arms around me. 'Let's go home.'

We walked through the fields, across the clearing and up the path towards the verandah. All the time Marysia was holding my hand and crying. Tears ran down her face on to her shawl. We walked up the steps and on to our verandah. I couldn't believe it. Panic rose in my throat. All the windows in the house were broken and the front door had been smashed in. I let go of Marysia's hand and walked inside. There were boot prints all over the floor. The air felt full of menace. Pictures and tapestries had been torn from the walls. I walked to the kitchen, keeping my arms at my sides, trying not to step on the splinters of wood and glass that littered the floor. The kitchen was a mess. Drawers had been pulled from the dresser and the contents dumped on the floor. Mama was standing there in the middle of the knives and spoons, forks and ladles with her mouth wide open, crying. It didn't seem like our home.

We stopped hiding out at night. Mama said that there was no point. We slept in our house with jagged glass in the windows and a broken door.

Always there were soldiers passing. We could see them from the verandah. The schools were closed. Feliks spent his days in the stable with the horses. I didn't know what to do. I couldn't play. Sometimes I helped Mama light huge bonfires with the papers that she brought from Tata's study. When there was nothing esle to do I hid behind the latticework on the verandah and watched the clouds of dust on the road coming closer and closer until they turned into men in uniform. I stared and stared, hoping that one of them might be Tata. Only he would be able to fight off the uneasiness that lurked around our house.

Everything was the same and yet so different. All day

soldiers tramped along the road with guns on their shoulders and packs on their backs. We knew that something would happen, and yet day by day life went on in the same way. The soldiers shouted to each other in a strange harsh language as they marched past our house.

'They are Russians,' Feliks said.

I stopped looking for Tata among them.

One evening a big column of soldiers turned off the road and started marching up the lane towards our house. I remember standing behind the latticework and seeing them coming. Instinctively I dropped to the verandah floor as the soldiers marched closer to the house. I wanted to tell Mama but I didn't want to let the soldiers see me.

Wriggling along the verandah floor I crept in through the broken door. Fear gripped me by the throat. Everything in our house seemd so precious and beautiful. Mama had a red and white striped kerchief over her head.

'What is the matter, Kryska?' she asked as I crawled through the door. 'You look so pale.'

I opened my mouth to speak but no words would come. Just a gasping noise from the back of my throat. Mama put down her black rags and helped me to sit down on the floor.

'Kryska,' she said, 'you must tell me what is happening.'

Marysia came hurrying in through the back door.

'Quick, Mama,' she said, tearing off her apron. 'The Russians are here.'

Mama closed her eyes for just a moment and her lips tightened. I knew that for weeks she had been expecting something like this to happen. 'Where is Feliks?' she asked Marysia.

'Here,' Feliks said. He was standing behind her, gripping an old rifle. Tata had kept it in the attic but after he left Feliks had brought the gun down and kept it beside his bed. He knew how to shoot. Tata had given him lessons since he was eleven years old.

I looked at my family. There was fear on their faces. Fear and dread. I scrambled up off the floor and crept behind the stove. I wanted to hide myself away in a place where no one would see me.

Mama took off her kerchief and smoothed her hair. I peered around the corner of the stove, watching her. She smoothed her skirt and walked through the makeshift front door to look out at the Russians. The sun was low in the sky. I knew that it would be shining straight in her eyes, dazzling her with its brightness.

The soldiers broke ranks as they came into our fields. They unpacked their haversacks and started plundering the woodshed for firewood. Soon there were fires on all sides of the house, burning with a strong steady light. We peered through the front door, watching them, Feliks with the gun, Mama, Marysia and I with our hands by our sides. We saw the soldiers run into the orchard. They tore branches from the trees and threw them on to the fires. Feliks's grip tightened on the gun but Mama held his arm and spoke to him quietly. There was not much a boy could do against so many men.

We watched until the sun went down and the evening

began to close. The men piled wood high on the fires so that the flames leapt and danced in front of our eyes. They trampled the fences and flattened the fields. As evening fell they surrounded the house and shouted, '*Dawajcie jesc, dawajcie jesc …*' It was a demand for food.

Mama left the doorway and walked to the kitchen. She moved so slowly, like a very old lady. Marysia and Feliks rushed to help her, Marysia calling me to hurry along. She opened the cupboards and loaded my arms with bread and pickles. She gave Feliks a huge bowl of freshly made yoghurt. We walked outside and put the food on the bottom of the steps. It wasn't enough. In two minutes the food was gone and the men were shouting for more. Mama opened all the cupboards and carried out our food. Jars of preserved fruit golden with summer sun, salted meat and sacks of potatoes. Soon we put the food on the verandah and the men grabbed it. We could smell potatoes baking in the fires. Mama gave Feliks the outdoor cellar key and told him to let the soldiers take all they wanted.

'But what about us?' Feliks asked. 'We need this food for winter.'

'May God save us,' Mama said in reply. I didn't understand what she meant but I didn't mind. All I wanted was for the soldiers to go away and leave us alone. I saw their guns and I was scared.

The soldiers ransacked the cellar, whooping as they discovered Tata's wine. And then they took Marysia, bursting in through the broken door and dragging her outside, tearing her hair and ripping her clothes. I screamed and shouted, howling at them to let her go. A soldier tore my dress and hit me across the face, laughing. He threw me across the room and my head bumped and banged along the floor. But I was still screaming, all the time screaming and shouting while Mama went crazy. She attacked the soldiers, scratching their faces and pummelling them with her fists.

'Let her go …' she was shouting. 'Leave my daughter!' The men laughed and pushed Mama to the floor. They kicked her face with their heavy boots … kicked her again and again until she was quiet. I bit my arm until it was bleeding. I closed my eyes and prayed. My mind was roaring. I had to stuff my fingers in my mouth and bite them hard to stop myself screaming. I didn't want the soldiers to notice me again. I didn't want them to hurt me like they were hurting my mother.

After a while the men seemed to lose interest in Mama. They left her lying there on the floor and went out the front door. I lay still for a while watching and waiting, wondering what had happened to Feliks. Then I crawled over to Mama. Her face was black and puffy but she was still breathing. She wasn't dead.

My head was hurting but I dragged myself upright and got some water from the bucket. I went to my bedroom and got a blanket. All the time I could hear myself crying, tight breathless sobs that seemed to have no end. And I could hear someone banging. It sounded as if they were shut up in the bread oven. I opened the oven door and there was Feliks, tied up tight. He fell towards me and I had to get a kitchen knife to slit the ropes. He hugged me tightly for just a minute and then went to look after Mama. I made a pillow for her head and Feliks covered her with the blanket. We didn't talk. There was nothing to be said.

In the dark the soldiers' presence surrounded us. A low rumbling noise came from their camp, the sound of hundreds of men talking. It rose and fell like the wind in the trees, ebbing and flowing with its own motion. It was the noise of men bringing doom, men without families herded together in army formation, marching to the will of those who directed their awesome power. They ate and drank, slashed and burned with a single-minded determination. Life and death were subordinate to the powerful will of war that directed their hand. I sat in the dark and thought about my sister Marysia, wondering if she was alive or dead.

In the dark of that long night came a terrible screeching.

Feliks rushed to the door. Mama opened her eyes. They were scared and bloodshot. She began to pray, mumbling familiar words through her swollen lips. Feliks stared out into the night which was lit by the twinkle of campfires.

'I think it is *moja swinka*,' he said. 'They have killed our pig.' I cried. I ran to my bedroom to stuff my head under the pillow, to shut out the sound of *moja swinka*'s agony. Her fat friendly snout was in front of my eyes. She was the only pig to escape poisoning. She was so tame she would eat delicately from your hand. I had known her for three years while she grew from the sweetest little piglet into a huge sow. She had her own pigsty behind the woodshed and every evening I fed her the food scraps. My pillow was soaked with tears. Feliks came and led me back into the kitchen.

'We must stay together,' he said.

The soldiers ate and sang till late at night. They built a huge spit in front of the house and roasted great hunks of *moja swinka*'s flesh. The smell of cooking meat was thick in the air and we heard the noise of the soldiers butchering other animals. Feliks and I took turns to bathe Mama's face. I fetched her clean clothes and helped her change, biting my lips to stop the tears falling. Feliks and I helped her off the floor. She sat in the rocking chair in the corner of the kitchen. I covered her with a white counterpane and brushed her hair. Outside we could hear rowdy bursts of singing and shouting. We sat in the kitchen together, all of us thinking about the Russian soldiers and our Marysia.

After a long time Mama stood up and walked out the door.

Feliks leapt after her. 'Mama!' he called.

She turned around. 'I must get her back,' she said softly through bruised lips.

'Then I will come with you,' Feliks said.

'You stay with Krystyna,' she said, and picking up the meat cleaver she walked down the steps into the night.

We stood in the doorway watching her. The night was still bright with smouldering firelight. Mama walked from bonfire to bonfire, staring at the groups of men clustered together, looking for her eldest daughter, calling her by name. The soldiers laughed and shouted after her, calling her names. But no one touched her. She walked from fire to fire with the meat cleaver tensed in her hands.

It seemed like a long time before she returned to the house, alone. Feliks and I were lying on the floor under a blanket. Mama sat in the chair rocking slowly backwards and forwards, backwards and forwards. I don't remember the rest of that night, but as the dawn came the soldiers started moving. Slowly the jumbled groups of men lying on the ground became an army again and Marysia walked in through the door. I got up and ran to her.

'No,' she said, pushing me away.

'Maryska,' Mama said softly. She was still sitting in the rocking chair.

Marysia huddled in a heap on the floor. Her lips were split and swollen. Her eyes were bruised and her clothes were filthy and torn. There was blood on her skirt, her hands and her face. But it was the look in her eyes that worried me most. My sister Marysia seemed to have gone. An empty face stared up at me. It was the face of a stranger.

The soldiers formed ranks and marched away, singing as they tramped down the road. Feliks and I watched through the cracks in the boarded-up door but Mama was on her knees, praying.

'Kneel down, children,' she said. 'We must thank God.' We knelt and prayed but I wanted to go outside. I wanted to see the hollows in the earth were the soldiers had lain to sleep. I wanted to poke around in the ashes of their fires. I wanted to find out what they had done to Marysia. Silence fell. Without the noise of the soldiers it was so quiet and still. I could barely remember it this quiet before. Feliks pushed open the front door.

'Argghh ...' Mama shrieked.

There in the middle of the verandah steps was *moja swinka*'s head.

The Soviet soldiers moved into our town. They closed the schools and boarded up the churches. They took the houses they wanted and pushed people out into the streets. Now there were hundreds of people on the road, walking with bundles and pushing carts loaded with their belongings. Mama helped anyone who knocked at our door.

'It could be us next,' she said when Feliks scolded her for letting another family have a bag of grain.

There were people camping out everywhere. In the mornings Mama heated gallons of water on the stove and with the help of Feliks lugged the cauldrons out on to the verandah for people who were camping in the forest. They came with cups and bowls, looking tired and worried. There were people from the village and strangers with their families. They took the hot water and scurried back to their hiding places. No one wanted to be caught by the Soviets and no one knew what would happen next.

We still had our home to ourselves. Every day I expected the soldiers to come and turn us out. I had said goodbye to the verandah steps, to my bed and to the little hazelnut tree that Tata had planted on the day I was born. Most of the day I sat on our steps and waited. Sometimes Marysia came and sat beside me. Her legs were covered with bruises and soundless sobbing shook her body and tore at my heart. I tried to hold her hand and kiss her face but she pushed me away.

'Don't touch me,' she said in a voice hoarse from crying.

I wished that I could hold her in my arms the way I remembered her holding me. Instead I sat beside my crying sister and stared out towards the forest.

People who passed our house offered snippets of news but no one knew exactly what was happening. Every two or three days Soviet soldiers would drive up and take food from our farm. They killed all the hens and drove away the heifers. One day they brought a large farm wagon and loaded it with grain from our cellar.

'Let them choke on it,' Mama said as we stood watching them from the verandah.

I hoped that they would take all the grain and leave us alone. Winter was coming and the soldiers started making registers.

They came to the door and asked us our names. They tramped through the house and looked in all the cupboards. One or two of them spoke a little Polish. They asked about Tata and what he was doing. Mama spoke to them bravely, without fear in her voice, but she kept a restraining arm on Feliks's shoulder. The soldiers made him angry when they helped themselves to the food in the kitchen and made notes about everything they saw on the farm.

Neighbours came to our house to talk about the registers. No one knew why the soldiers were writing everything down. Every day there were women sitting in our kitchen, sighing and wringing their hands. We had no coffee left but Mama served *herbata* and made flat cakes without butter or sugar which tasted like a sort of doughy bread. Feliks and I helped Mama to serve the visitors but these were not like the joyful visits of the past. No one noticed the food they ate. No one laughed or smiled. There was fear in the air as the women talked and drank Mama's tea. I wondered what would happen next.

The goods in the shops vanished. There was nothing to buy, not even a comb. People everywhere were being stripped of what they owned. Grain, food, livestock, even the machinery in factories was being seized as the property of the Soviet Union.

Mama decided to go into Baranowiczie to see what was happening. I begged and pleaded with her not to go. I was afraid that as soon as she walked out of my sight she would be gone. My tears had no effect. Mama dressed carefully in an old dress and coat. She covered her head with a shawl and then visited our neighbours to borrow some eggs. She wanted to carry something in a basket in case she was stopped on the road. She arranged the three precious eggs in a basket covered with straw, then she looked at each of us carefully and asked Feliks if he would come with her. Of course he agreed. Being with Mama seemed safer than being left alone.

I swallowed my tears as they walked down the lane and on to the road. 'Goodbye Mama, goodbye Feliks,' I whispered. I stood and watched them walking until they were just small specks in the distance, wondering if I would ever see them again.

There were Russian soldiers everywhere on the road.

Mama held her little basket of eggs close by her side so that they would not be broken. Feliks walked steadily beside her. Neither of them spoke a word. As they reached the village where I went to school they were stopped by soldiers.

'Name?' asked the soldier as he stepped out into the middle of the road. He did not look at Mama's face. He did not look at her at all. She was like some sort of irritating non-presence in front of him. Another Pole.

Mama leaned heavily on Feliks's shoulder. 'My name is Ludmilla,' she said. 'And this is my son Feliks.' She spoke clearly and look straight ahead. Only Feliks knew that she was scared. Her fingers were digging into the back of his neck.

The soldiers surrounded them, making a crowd right in the middle of the road. People passing kept their distance and looked away. One of the soldiers helped himself to an egg out of Mama's basket. Feliks clenched his teeth. He looked up and the soldier was staring at him. Feliks dropped his gaze to the ground. The egg splattered on to his shoe. The soldier helped himself to another. Now there was only one egg left.

'You can go,' said the soldier with the list, and he moved on.

'Are you making a list so that you can take us all to Siberia?' Mama asked as he brushed past her.

The soldier with the list spat in the dust. 'We don't want you Poles anywhere in our country,' he said, 'not even in Siberia.'

Feliks and Mama returned home with their one egg. Mama was pale and silent. She drank tea and lay on her bed with her eyes closed. She seemed to have some sort of fever.

I moistened her forehead with cloths soaked in cold water. She lay quite still but I knew she was not sleeping. When I took her hand in mine she clenched my fingers so hard it hurt. Feliks covered her with a feather quilt.

'Mama is tired out,' he said. 'We will let her rest. Things will be different in the morning.'

There was no morning. In the middle of the night the soldiers came. I woke to the sound of Mama screaming and crying. Marysia came rushing into my room. Her feet made a thundering sound on the floor.

'Quickly, Kryska,' she said, 'get dressed. Put on everything you can.'

I climbed out of bed but I felt as if I was still dreaming.

Somewhere in the back of my head I could hear Mama crying, sobbing as if her heart was breaking.

It was cold. I could see my breath in front of my face and I knew that winter was near. Soon it would snow and the fields outside would be smothered by a freezing white blanket. It seemed hard to get dressed. My hands were shaking. I put on two pairs of woollen stockings, two dresses and a knitted shawl. Then I put on my padded over-trousers. I felt so fat and clumsy I could hardly walk. I took a deep breath and said goodbye to my bedroom. I sat on my bed and traced the words that Dziadek had carved on my bedhead. Then I walked out of my room.

The house was full of soldiers with guns by their sides. I could hear Mama crying, and outside the dogs were barking loudly.

'Silence them,' the NKVD officer said. One of the soldiers marched outside. There were two shots. The dogs stopped barking.

'Thirty minutes,' the NKVD officer was saying. 'You have thirty minutes before you leave.'

His words fell as blows in the silence of the room. I could vaguely hear Mama sobbing. Marysia was rummaging through the kitchen cupboards, stuffing things into an old saddlebag. Like an overdressed dummy I stood there in the middle of the kitchen, wondering what to do. Half an hour! The minutes were ticking away before my eyes. Soon there would only be twenty minutes left.

What would you do if the soldiers came into your home and said that they were taking you away? Destination unknown. What would you take? A spoon and fork? A bar of soap and a piece of bread?

I turned and ran to my room, rifling through the cupboard for my Sunday dress. I was already wearing two dresses, but suddenly it became very important to have my best one with me. I took my feather pillow and the straw doll that Auntie Danuta had given me. I felt panicky and feverish, searching, looking, grabbing at things that I had lived with all my eight years, trying to take my life with me.

Mama was walking up and down the hall, wailing and crying like a crazy woman. She was pulling things from cupboards, emptying drawers and all the time Feliks was following her, picking up bundles, packing clothes, collecting photographs and Tata's remaining papers, putting everything in a sack. I wanted to help him but my feet seemed frozen to the floor. I stood with my untidy bundles in the doorway of my room until Marysia came to find me.

'Quickly, Kryska, come and help me with the bread.' She grabbed my hand and led me down to the kitchen. 'Now make a pile by the door,' she said, climbing up behind the stove and passing down the sacks of dried bread that Mama had stored there. I struggled with the heavy, unwieldy sacks, but it felt good to be helping Marysia, as if the work blotted out the fear.

The soldiers were impatient. At first they had stood still, silent and watchful. But Mama's wailing seemed to annoy them. 'Tell her to be quiet,' the NKVD officer said to Feliks. But Feliks could do nothing to soothe Mama. Every part of the house filled with the sound of her sorrowing. Now there were only ten minutes left. Feliks started stuffing things from the pile into our suitcases. There was so much to take. How could we choose what to leave behind?

The soldiers moved around the house. The end of our time was coming. Already our house had lost its familiar shape. Everyone was rooting around grabbing things. Nothing seemed to make sense. One of the soldiers climbed up on to the kitchen table and wrenched the carved crucifix off the wall. He threw it to the floor where the dark wood splintered and tore.

I was eight years old. It was hard to understand what was happening. I wished that Mama would stop crying. The sudden awakening, the soldiers, the feverish packing, the crucifix smashing down on to the floor … all these things passed so quickly before my eyes that none of them seemed real.

A soldier started rummaging through the pile of things that we had collected at the door, throwing aside shoes, rugs and Mama's evening dress. Feliks shouldered him aside.

'Leave them alone,' he shouted. 'You have everything else. These things are ours.'

The soldier hit Feliks across the face. Whap! The sound of the slap was so loud that for a moment Mama stopped crying. Another soldier grabbed Feliks and tied him to the back of a chair.

'Polish dog,' he spat and hit Feliks hard on the other side of the face. Now Mama was screaming and Feliks was shouting. Blood from his nose was running down the front of his face. 'Be strong,' he was saying. 'Stay together …'

The sound of his voice saying those same words over and over calmed me down. I stood and watched while the NKVD officer checked everything in our bags. Speaking in a rough sort of Polish, he read a list of things that we were permitted to take from our home. Clothing, bedding, kitchen utensils and enough food to last for a month. The total was not to exceed one hundred kilos. The soldiers counted and weighed all our possessions. Anything that did not meet with their approval was tossed aside. Watching these strangers handle our things was like being dispossessed. The fabric of our lives was sorted without a thought for those who would wear the clothes, without concern as to whether the food would last. It was enough for the soldiers to follow the items on the list and to clear out the house within half an hour.

*Chapter 2*

The weighing and sorting was completed. We stood at the door of our home with an approved one hundred kilograms of possessions. At the order of the NKVD officer we left our house, walking down the familiar verandah steps, walking and crying, dragging our belongings with us.

It was dark outside, some time before the light of dawn. The air was clean and cold. Frost covered the earth and glittered brightly in the moonlight. The stillness of the night was broken by the scrunching of our footsteps on the frozen ground and Mama's broken sobbing.

The soldiers followed us down the lane, holding their guns in front of them. Our procession was led by the NKVD officer who walked quickly, shouting at us to keep up. I walked in between my mother and my sister, trying to see through the tears that were flooding down my face. My throat ached from crying and my heart seemed to be thumping too loudly in my chest.

At the end of the lane our farm wagon stood ready. Our own horses were standing there in the harness and they whinnied as we came closer. I wondered if they thought it was strange to be harnessed by unfamiliar hands in the middle of the night. I wanted to ask the soldiers where they were taking us but my tongue stuck to the roof of my mouth and I was silent.

The soldiers surrounded the wagon. With a nod of his head the NKVD officer indicated that we were to climb in. I scrambled up without hesitating. In the dark the soldiers seemed menacing and it seemed safer to do what they wanted. Mama was crying and crying. I helped her to sit down and arranged her coat around her knees, but she didn't seem to notice. She was sobbing and calling on God in heaven to save us and our home. Marysia handed up our bundles and bags, and together we heaved the sacks of grain up on to the cart. Then she stopped and spoke to the NKVD officer, asking him what would happen to our brother.

The officer seemed surprised to hear Marysia speaking. Perhaps he did not realise that we were living people whom he was loading on to the cart. He did not seem to hear Mama wailing and crying, and he stared at Marysia as if she was a talking post. I was frightened again. Marysia looked so small and vulnerable standing there. I had to stuff my hands into my mouth to stop myself from shouting. I wanted to do something to save her from the sharp gaze of the NKVD officer. He seemed to narrow his eyes and then pointed up the lane.

'Your brother is coming,' he said in Polish and gave Marysia a push towards the wagon.

Feliks was led down the lane by a soldier who indicated that he was to climb up on to the wagon. His hands were tied, so Marysia and I hauled him up by the shoulders. As soon as he was sitting there with us, Mama stopped crying. For a minute or two it didn't seem to matter that we were being dispossessed of our home and our land. The most important thing was that we were all together, whatever our destination.

Things started moving. The NKVD officer was sitting in front of us, holding the reins. Our faithful horses took up the pace, just as they did in the fields. We clung together and stared into the night trying to see our home for as long as we could. The front door was wide open and the windows were broken. It seemed as if the life had gone out of it.

We bumped down the farm track and reached the main road. Although it was dark, it was crowded with wagons and carts, horses and trucks. On all the corners there were Soviet soldiers moving the traffic along, hustling the horses to move faster. I had never seen so many people travelling on this road, even during the day. Joining the mainstream of traffic, we pulled in alongside another farm wagon like ours.

'Move along,' shouted the soldier who was driving with us.

He jostled the horses so that we were riding alongside

the next cart. I looked across at it, trying to see who else was being driven away from their home, but all I could see were the outlines of people with their belongings piled up around them. In the darkness they looked like everyone else to me. It was Mama who recognised them.

'Anna!' she called. Her voice was muffled by the creaking of the wagons, the soldiers' shouting and the clattering of the carts on the road. But I knew who it was. Anna Petrovka, our neighbour. I loved going to her house because she made such good honeycake. On the wagon alongside us her two daughters stared out like owls in the night. These girls were my heroes. They could jump from the woodshed roof and cross the stream when it was covered with crackling ice. I waved and shouted but they just stared back. There was a gap in the traffic and their wagon moved ahead of ours. I wonder where they are now.

There were hundreds of people on the road that night. The traffic made a solid, moving tide. There were even people walking and carrying their huge bundles, hurried on by the soldiers with guns. We turned right and then left. Soon we knew where we were heading.

'The railway station,' Feliks said.

We all sat closer. Feliks held my hand but he was watching Mama. 'Don't cry,' he kept saying. 'We will need to be ready.' Mama sobbed on and on.

You can't imagine what it was like. People and carts and soldiers and wagons were everywhere. Horses were rearing in distress. People were shouting and crying. Soldiers were pulling and pushing and shoving, forcing bottlenecks of people on to the railway station. There were women and children, babies in their mothers' arms and old people who had to be carried. Women were screaming, boys were fighting, pushing up against the soldiers. The noise was deafening. It was as if the gates of hell had been opened. And then it was our turn.

The horses stopped and the NKVD officer climbed down. He walked around to the back of the wagon and shouted, 'Get down.' We shrank back, not wanting to leave the safety of our wagon, even though it offered no protection. Somehow I felt a sort of link with the NKVD officer. He had been in our home. He had called us from our beds. The wagon and the officer were the only reminders of home in this awful place of screaming and crying. We all sat there, still and silent, sitting on the wagon that Dziadek had made. I wished that we could go home.

The soldiers were impatient. 'Get down!' shouted the officer. Feliks was the first to move. He leapt to the ground and started passing down our bags. The moment of safety had passed. Now we were to be part of the milling mass of people being pushed on to the station. I jumped to the ground while Marysia gave Mama a helping hand.

'Quick,' said Feliks, 'unload the bags. Soon they will drive the wagon away.'

I heaved and pulled, dragging our things to the ground.

Marysia and Mama worked beside me. We worked fast but Feliks was right. As soon as there was a gap in the traffic the soldiers drove away with our wagon and horses. There was a sack of grain and a bundle of our bedding still on the back. Mama started shouting and cursing the soldiers. Feliks folded his arms around her.

'Don't worry, Mama,' he said. 'It is gone and we must concentrate on keeping together.'

Even as Feliks was talking people were banging against us. We were being pushed and buffeted on all sides as people were forced towards the station. Children were stumbling and being trampled on the ground. Old people were being knocked down. I clenched my teeth and held a bundle in each hand. Feliks tied a sack on to my back. He did the same for Mama and Marysia. We moved closer together, walking slowly, weighed down by our things. People pushed around us as soldiers hustled those on the edge of the crowd. I kept my eyes fixed on Marysia's back. I knew that if I fell over I would lose my family for ever.

The noise of the crowd rose in waves around us. Such crying and screaming and praying. You never heard anything like it. As we came closer to the great gates of Baranowiczie Station, I could see rows and rows of Soviet soldiers standing to attention with their guns at their sides.

There was only one gate through which you could gain entrance to the station platform. Soviet officers were standing on either side of it, checking names off huge thick lists. The crowd was being pushed towards that narrow gate. You could feel the people behind you pressing closely. It was like being shunted towards the gate of the damned.

'Family name?' the officer shouted as we came within hearing.

Feliks stated all our names. The officer marked them on the list with a thick black pencil. It meant nothing to him, we were just lines on a page, but for those of us named there the lists detailed the end of the lives we had known. As we passed through the station gate we were counted. Nobodies. Poles without faces, without names, without homes. Numbers on lines, lines on a page. I held tightly to the back of Marysia's coat as we went through the gate. The surging roar of the crowd rose to meet us. The desperation, the distress, the sobbing and crying were even worse than the chaos outside.

There seemed to be something happening at the front of the platform. I craned my neck to see but there was nothing around me but the press of people's backs and the sharp edges of their bags and bundles. We shuffled forwards. Then, from the edge of the crowd, a word rippled towards us. Mouths hung open as they heard the word.

'Ciepluszki ... ciepluszki ...' You could feel terror in the air. Beside me, Marysia was shivering. She kept on and on repeating that word in funny jerky phrases. 'Cie ... plus ... zki ...'

Feliks was standing just in front of her. He managed to turn around against the press of the crowd and to look at Marysia. His arms were loaded with our things but he leaned forward and shouted into Marysia's face. 'Stop it! Don't think about it! Close your eyes and think of something else instead.'

There was so much happening around me, so many people shrieking and crying that I didn't really take it in. I didn't know what they meant by *ciepluszki* and it didn't matter until Mama went crazy, dropping her suitcase, tearing out huge handfuls of hair and screaming at the top of her voice.

'Mama!' Feliks shouted. He dropped his bundles and threw his arms around her. Mama put her head on Feliks's shoulder and wept.

Slowly we edged towards the platform and I saw the things that they were talking about. *Ciepluszki* were cattle wagons. There were thirty or forty of them drawn up in a long line. The huge doors were open and soldiers were pushing people inside. When the wagon was stuffed full, the doors were slammed shut and bolted on the outside.

I felt numb. All around me people were screaming and praying, cursing and crying. My stomach churned with fear. It would be dark inside those wagons. There were only two very small windows right at the top, under the roof.

Then it was our turn to stand in front of the gaping door. Feliks leapt inside, dragging our things after him. Sacks of bread, suitcases, bundles of clothes and our feather *pijiny*. Mama was shrieking and fighting as the soldiers hauled her into the wagon. I started to climb up the small steps into the gloomy darkness when Marysia, who was right behind me, tripped and fell to the ground.

'Feliks!' I shouted.

He grabbed my bundles and I jumped down to help Marysia.

A soldier hauled me up by the neck. I could hardly breathe. I tried to tell him about Marysia but he just threw me into the wagon. I landed with a thud against the bodies of people already inside. Someone landed against me. It was Marysia. Then the darkness and chaos closed in around me. Marysia was lost again. Women were screaming, men were shouting. More and more people were pressed into the wagon and the door was slammed shut. It was completely dark inside. You could not see your neighbour whose nose was right beside your face. I wished that I could go home. Somewhere near me a woman started to pray.

There was just enough room to stand. Hundreds of people were packed into that small space. There was nothing else, just a mass of living bodies, a layer of wooden shelves along one wall and a chimney sticking up through the middle of the roof. It was suffocatingly close.

After a while, your eyes became used to the darkness. People began shuffling round a bit, trying to make more room. All around you could hear fragments of conversation. People were talking about their homes, about what they had left behind, about what would happen to us now. I wished that I could stand beside Marysia. I wanted to feel Feliks's strength near me. It was impossible to walk forwards. But I was small. Crouching down on my hands and knees I crawled through the forest of legs on the floor. People twitched and kicked out at me but I kept crawling, looking for the legs that I had grown up beside.

The wagon was hot, dark and noisy. Everyone was talking at once so you couldn't yell out and be heard. Sometimes there were small gaps between the legs and I stopped to listen to the conversations above me, trying to hear voices that were familiar.

At first I imagined that I heard the voice of Auntie Danuta.

She was Mama's sister and my favourite aunt. I wanted to call out to her, 'Here I am, Auntie,' just like I did in her garden when I jumped out to give her a fright. Here in the wagon things were different. No one would hear if I shouted. No one listened to all the weeping and wailing. I lay still among the legs and strained to hear what the Auntie Danuta voice was saying.

'Listen, please,' she was shouting. 'Only God knows what will happen to us now. We must take care of each other.'

Then I knew that it was her. For a moment I revelled in the sound of her rich deep voice. I remembered how we loved going to stay with her in Vilno, at the house which had belonged to our grandparents. We would stand and stare at the dim brown photographs of Dziadek and Babchia with two little girls standing beside them. 'That's Danuta and me,' Mama would say. It was strange to think that Mama had once been a girl.

'We have to make the best of what is happening to us…' Auntie Danuta was saying. 'We need more room to move. The old people and the sick, they should lie on those *prycze*, the shelves on the side of the wagon …'

Unbelievably, people started shuffling around doing what Auntie Danuta had suggested. Old *babchias* who should have been sitting beside the stove at home edged their way across the wagon towards the wooden shelves.

Others moved aside so that they could get past.

'Mothers with babies and pregnant women should lie on the second layer of *prycze*,' Auntie Danuta said. The resonance of her beautiful voice was cracked with tears, but people were slowly moving to do what she urged. A *prycze* was not a comfortable bed. The plank shelves had no covering and the space between them was not high enough for a person to sit upright, but at least it was a place to lie down. There was a stilling of that blind sense of panic.

I took advantage of the shifting crowd to scramble forwards.

I wanted to see Auntie Danuta more clearly. I wanted to touch her, to hold her hand. I could remember so clearly our visit to her estate when we had sung and danced at the *dozynki*. Auntie Danuta had worn a beautiful cornflower-blue dress that matched the colour of her eyes. Now in the dim light Danuta looked old and tired. Her blonde hair was coiled in the plait that she always wore when she went to bed. She was weeping even while she was helping a very old lady to scramble up on to the lower level of the *prycze*.

'Auntie Danuta!' I yelled.

All of a sudden I was afraid that I would always be lost, crawling around on the floor of the wagon. My heart was pounding and I heard myself screaming, felt myself pushing and kicking against the people around me. Then gentle hands were holding me still. Strong hands were passing me through the crowd to Auntie Danuta. She clasped me in her arms, kissing me over and over again until we were both laughing and kissing, our tears drenching each other's face.

Danuta reached into her pocket and brought out a tiny sprig of lavender.

'Smell,' she said and thrust it right under my nose. I sniffed hard through my tears and the smell brought back a feeling of security. It was the smell of the bedrooms at Auntie Danuta's house where every bed was made with a bunch of lavender under the pillow.

'And now we must find your mother,' my aunt said, drying her eyes on her sleeve. 'I suppose you're not the only one in your family to end up in this God-forsaken place.'

I nodded and smiled and held tight to Auntie Danuta's hand as she began pushing her way through the crowd, peering closely at people as she passed them. I knew that Mama was in there somewhere and I followed along looking for the familiar bundles we had brought with us. Then Auntie Danuta stopped abruptly beside a woman who was squatting on the ground, half hidden by her husband.

'Please — stop,' she said. 'We can't just squat anywhere. The filth will kill us and we are not animals to urinate where we stand.'

The woman's husband was angry. 'But Pani,' he said, 'where can we go? They have locked us inside this wagon and they will not open to our knocking.'

Auntie Danuta sighed. I held on to her hand, watching and listening. It had not occurred to me that there was nowhere to go to the toilet. Just thinking about it made me need to go.

'Over here,' a voice said from somewhere near the back of the wagon. 'There's a hole in the floor.'

As soon as he spoke the crowd surged in his direction.

Everyone was pushing and shoving, trying to get a look at that hole. I held even tighter to Auntie Danuta as we pressed towards the man who had found the hole. People trod on my feet and elbowed my head. They were desperate to get out of this box, and the hole seemed to promise an escape. But the hole was tiny. Even a very small person would have trouble squeezing through it. Yet down there on the bottom was the glimmer of daylight and the glimpse of a tiny fragment of railway track.

'Let me through, let me through,' a man was shouting. He pushed his way to the front of the crowd around the hole and knelt down to climb in. There was an air of desperation about him. People moved away to give him more space, trying not to look as he grunted and heaved, trying to push his body down through the hole in the floor. It was much too small. Perhaps a child like me could have squeezed through, but I clung to Auntie Danuta and put the thought out of my mind.

Defeated at last, the man dragged himself back on to his feet and edged away into the crowd. His place at the hole was taken by an older man who pulled a small knife from his pocket and started hacking away at the wooden floor, trying to make the hole bigger. Swearing and cursing, he sawed on and on, breathless with excitement. People stood around the hole watching him. There was no other way to pass the time except to stare into the darkness.

After a while an old white-haired man tapped Danuta on the arm.

'Forgive me, Pani,' he said, 'but my wife, she urgently needs to …' and he indicated the hole in the floor.

My aunt looked at the man sawing feverishly at the edges of the hole and sighed. Anyone could see that the idea of escape was hopeless. The knife was so small it would be worn out before the hole was big enough for a grown man to get through.

'Listen,' Danuta said to the man scrabbling at the hole, 'even if you make this hole big enough they will shoot you as soon as you get outside. At least while we are in this wagon we are alive, maybe we have some chance of living.'

Those who were standing around the hole muttered their agreement.

'Let us try and make things bearable,' said a grey-haired man. '*Tak*,' a woman agreed. 'We need somewhere to go, otherwise the shit will be running all over the floor and the Russians won't care if we die in here.'

People were pushing closer and closer to the hole, watching and waiting. They seemed to be ready to act, to do something to the man who was so desperately sawing away there. He looked up and sensed their impatience.

'All right, all right,' he muttered, stuffing his knife back into his pocket. 'Go on then, use this for your piss-hole. I will think of something else.' He stepped backwards into the crowd which parted to make room for him, and Auntie Danuta stepped forward to take his place.

'This will be our toilet,' she said. 'Perhaps we can arrange some sort of privacy.'

Almost immediately a woman came forward with a

linen tablecloth. 'Please,' she said, 'I would like to offer this cloth. Perhaps we can hang it somehow.' And then she started to tell the story of how she was taken from her home in the middle of the night.

Soon other women pushed through the crowd carrying sheets and even curtains. They all told the same story of being woken in the middle of the night by Russian soldiers. There was panic in their voices and I could sense their fear of our unknown future. No one knew where we were going or if we'd leave the wagon alive.

A small quietly spoken man tapped Auntie Danuta on the shoulder. 'Pani,' he said, 'I am a carpenter. Perhaps I can help.'

He brought a handful of nails from his pocket and jammed them between the cracks in the wall. Using the back of his heavy boot he hammered the nails into the wall and then stretched the sheets and tablecloths across the corner so that the toilet hole was covered. Now we had somewhere private to relieve ourselves.

The carpenter was the hero of the moment. Everyone was reaching out to clap him on the back, and for a few moments there were smiles on people's faces instead of tears. This small act seemed like a victory to us.

Suddenly the train started moving, shunting forwards two or three hundred yards and then jolting to a halt on a siding. We waited on that siding for two or three days. It was easy to lose track of the time. Nothing marked the passing of the hours except the noises from the station. Peering through the tiniest cracks in the walls we watched and waited. Our wagon was guarded twenty-four hours a day. During daylight hours the soldiers thumped on the wagon walls, shouting to us to stay silent. People muttered that they were trying to hide the fact that the wagons held humans and not cattle.

We took turns lying down on the top *prycze*, but when my turn came it was hard to sleep. Every muscle in my body was aching. I closed my eyes and suddenly the noise of so many people living there in the darkness engulfed me. Perhaps I slept for a few hours ... I don't know. I remember Feliks shaking me because it was his turn to lie on the *prycze*. I climbed back down to the floor, taking care not to step on the outstretched hands and legs of the people lying below me.

Once a day the soldiers slid open the wagon door and shoved in a large can of water. They then shouted, 'Bring out the dead.' People stood aside, pressing back against each other. There was a miserable little shuffling procession as two or three people carried out a body. An old woman ... two or three old men ... and once a child. That really frightened me. I hated shutting my eyes in that wagon because I was afraid that I would never wake up.

At first people fought for the can of water that the soldiers brought. It spilled on the floor as women clamoured to get enough for their children, and men pushed others aside while they filled whatever utensils they had. Mama urged Danuta to help people organise.

'But why?' Auntie Danuta asked. 'There is not enough water anyway. Maybe it is better to die now.'

Mama was shocked. She grabbed her sister by the shoulders and shook her hard. 'Danuta,' she said. 'Don't let it get you by the throat. Don't despair.' But Danuta just sat there, slumped on the floor, with her head in her hands. I had never seen her like that before.

It was Mama who made sure that everyone had a half cupful of water. She stood by the doors when they were rolled aside and took the can of water from the soldiers before a drop could spill on the floor. With a cup from our home, she dealt out the water until it was gone. There was just enough to moisten your lips and ease the ache in the back of your throat. In three gulps it was gone. And then there was another long thirsty day and night until the next water issue.

People settled into the endless stretches of time in the wagon but there was always a muted panic, a feeling of uneasiness about what would happen to us next. We could not wait for the train to begin moving, and yet we did not want to leave our home town. Here at least they gave us water.

There was nothing to eat except the supplies we had brought with us. Even in the shocked disorientation of our last few minutes at home, we had managed to bring dried bread, dried apples and some salted meat. Others had grabbed sacks of grain, oats and onions. But not everyone had been able to drag a sack of dried bread with them. Some had been rushed from their beds without any time to grab more than a handful of clothes; others had brought money and possessions to barter, believing that they would be able to buy food or bribe the guards wherever they were taken. Food became a preoccupation. I would sit there in the darkness thinking of Mama's golden yeast cake studded with plump raisins and her *pierogi* smothered with a thick mushroom sauce. For the first time in my life I was hungry all the time.

Mama was very careful with the food that we had brought. Every day she gave us some dried bread, a handful of dried apples and, at first, a tiny piece of bacon fat. By the third or fourth day the bacon fat was finished. She shared our dried bread with anyone who had come without. It was hard to watch her groping in the sack and giving away our food. I wondered what would happen when there was nothing at all left. Would we all starve here in this wooden box, clawing at the doors?

I tried to say these things to Auntie Danuta. I wanted to talk to her, to see her smile and laugh again, but she just sat on the floor and didn't seem to notice what was happening. Mama guided her over to the *prycze* and helped her to lie down, making a mattress out of a wad of clothes. People brought things for her, an apple or a lump of sugar. Danuta had stood up so bravely in the tumultuous early hours of our life in the wagon that by now everyone knew her. Mama steeped a handful of her special herbs in Danuta's water. She drank but she still did not talk. Mama said that Danuta was suffering from shock. It would be better if we did not worry.

There was nothing to do except stand or crouch on the floor and wait for your turn to lie down. Every two or three hours I had to fight down a terrible feeling of suffocation. It was hard to get used to being shut away from daylight and sunshine. I thought of our home and wondered what Tata would think when he came back from the war and found that we were gone. Sometimes we heard a surge of screaming and crying outside the wagon. Then we knew for sure that it was the middle of the night. You could hear the soldiers shouting and the people wailing as they were loaded into wagons like ours. Now and then we heard rifle shots. Then everyone was quiet and all you could see were the eyes of the people next to you staring into the darkness.

'Maybe they are going to shoot all of us,' a man said quietly.

His voice seemed to bring Auntie Danuta back from the dead. She stood up and lifted her hands high over her head. 'God is with us,' she said. 'Whether we live or die we will be Polish for ever.'

And then the train started moving. There was a series of sharp jolting motions forwards and backwards, forwards and backwards, so that people fell on top of one another. The wheels clanked on the rails and the couplings creaked as the wagons slowly picked up motion.

It was chaotic inside the wagon. The roll of the wheels on the rails was deafening. People were weeping or shouting. Some were hammering on the door with their fists, begging the soldiers to let us out. The wagon was moving so jerkily it was hard to stand upright. I fell on to the people beside me and then heaved myself to my feet and staggered over to stand by Mama.

'Where are we going?' I shouted to her. 'What will happen to us?'

She stood swaying with the movement of the wagon, tears falling down her face. The terrible noise of sobbing and crying was so loud and so sad that I could hardly bear it. No one answered my questions. Mama, Danuta and Marysia clung together. I held tight to Mama's skirt. I didn't know where we were going. I didn't know what would happen next.

After a while I got used to the noise of the wagon on the railway track. Our destination no longer mattered. I stood beside Marysia, trying to keep my aching body upright until it was my turn to lie down on the *prycze*. My throat was parched and my stomach taut with hunger. I waited and waited for the next cupful of water and hunk of dried bread.

The box-like wagon rumbled and swayed for days on end. Then suddenly it slammed to a halt. Everyone was thrown together, one on top of the other. The soldiers slid open the wooden doors and brought in water. People craned their necks to look outside, to see where we were, but nothing except empty fields stretched in front of us. There was the familiar call to bring out the dead and then the door was slammed shut and bolted again on the outside.

I longed to be able to run outside and look at the sky, to feel the sun on my face and my feet on the ground. Sometimes the train would stop for days on end. Nowhere. We lived without thinking about the life we had lost. All you wanted was for things to be better tomorrow.

Auntie Danuta had recovered but she was still very grave.

She edged around the wagon helping women with children, soothing sick people and encouraging the old to steady themselves, but sometimes she would sit on the floor with her hands over her face. I knew that she was crying.

Marysia was sunk in some private hell. She crouched in a heap with her legs tucked under her, slowly pulling hairs from her head and putting them into a sack.

There was no water for washing. The smell of so many people living closely together was heavy and fetid. Our hands and faces, necks and feet were smudged and grimy. Mama spent a lot of time combing hair. She often undid her long plaits and carefully teased the knots out of them. Then when they were replaited she turned her attention to me and Marysia. At home I wore my hair in two plaits looped together with ribbons. Here there were no ribbons and I only had one plait. Mama knotted it tightly. Her hands were not the hands she had at home. Now they were rough and impatient. She jerked my hair as she plaited it, all the time urging me to stand still.

'Why bother?' asked a woman who was watching.

Mama turned to look at her, yanking my plait really hard. 'If I don't bother my daughter will get lice,' she said. 'Hah!' the woman said, tossing her head. 'If lice is all she gets you can count yourself lucky.'

'Be quiet,' Mama said. 'Do not frighten the child.'

'She has eyes. She can see,' the woman continued. 'And

she will be watching the things that happen in this wagon.' 'Don't talk nonsense,' Mama said, pulling my plait even tighter. 'They have taken our homes but we are not dying.' The woman persisted. 'What is life in this wagon? You can't call it living.'

'There is hope,' Mama said and turned her back on the woman, concentrating fiercely on plaiting my hair.

All around me the adults were talking about what would happen, about where we were going and about the future of Poland. There were arguments and fights. Nerves were strained by the uncertainty. There were some who tried to interpret our future positively, while others were prophets of doom. After a while I could recognise different voices in the darkness — the deep scratchy voice of Pan Szymanowski who launched bitter tirades against the Soviets and the slow ponderous voice of Pan Cebulski who weighed up every incident with careful precision.

It was a new voice in the dark, the voice of Pan Lipinski, which suggested that we build a ladder so that we could look out of the little barred windows at the top of the wagon. Suddenly the idea of being able to look out and see the stars at night seemed like the most desirable thing in the world. The word passed around quickly. Imaginations were fired. People pushed through the crowd to contribute things dragged from their bundles — woollen stockings, linen tablecloths, skirts and shirts were all offered in the hope of making the ladder stronger. But Pan Lipinski looked at the pile of clothing and shook his head.

'We need to make sure that it does not rip or tear,' he

said. 'And when the train is moving the ladder must be strong enough to withstand the jolting and swaying.'

Some women started knotting stockings and blankets together, but when Pan Lipinski tested its strength the makeshift rope fell apart with the pressure of half his weight. The whole idea seemed hopeless until an elderly man emerged through the crowd.

'Excuse me please,' he said, 'perhaps I could offer this?' And he held out a coil of heavy rope.

A cheer rippled through the wagon. Now we would be able to reach the high windows in safety. Pan Lipinski took hold of the rope and held the old man in a close embrace.

'Thank you,' he said. 'We all thank you.' Then he expertly tied a ladder through the length of the rope and threw the end of the coil around the bars of the little window. The owner of the rope stood watching.

'I always bring my rope with me,' he said shyly. 'If we ever get out of here I would like to have it back.'

Pan Lipinski knotted the final rungs in the rope ladder and tested them for strength. 'It is ready,' he said. 'We will give the owner of the rope the first turn.'

'No … no,' the old man said, standing back. 'I am too stiff to climb all the way up there. You go first.'

Pan Lipinski climbed up the ladder to the small barred window. Everyone watched, craning their necks to see what would happen. For the first time I could remember the wagon was silent except for the creaking and groaning of the timber and the thundering of the wheels on the rails. We all stood and waited to hear about what Pan

Lipinski could see outside.

'I can see snow,' he called down to us, 'and land stretching for miles. But I cannot tell where we are.'

People crowded towards the ladder, anxious to take a turn and look outside the confines of the wagon. I joined the line and then it was my turn. I grabbed the ladder and climbed, trying to steady myself as the train began taking a corner in the track. The window was more than twenty steps up, and as soon as I reached the top I stuck my head between the bars and stared out. The air was fresh, crisp and clean, so unlike the air in the wagon. Ahead of me, rounding the corner in the track, were eighteen or twenty wagons that all looked exactly the same. Banked up against the tracks were huge drifts of snow. I held on with one hand and stuck my arm through the bars, aching to feel the cold wet touch of snow. The cold air and the glimpse of the wagons ahead excited me. Suddenly, I was sure we would survive. We were being taken to live, not die, somewhere, and with my lungs still full of the fresh cold air, I persuaded Mama to join the line and climb up the ladder. She clung awkwardly to the rope, scrabbling from foothold to foothold, but when she reached the top her hands clenched the bars and she stared out. For a while she was silent, gazing out with her face pressed to the bars. And then she started sobbing. 'Mama,' I shouted up to her, 'what is it? What can you see?' 'It's the border,' she called, 'I can see the boundary posts and the fences. We are passing across the border into Russia.' Mama's news was passed quickly from person to person and from the depths of the wagon came a terrible wailing, a sound so piteous that its echoes still turn my heart. Then someone started singing songs that told of our love for Poland. It was like the chorus of the saddest choir. Everyone was singing and crying and praying as we crossed the border into the Soviet Union.

Chapter 3

Life, death and darkness merged. People were going insane. There was never enough room to ease the pain in your legs. There was never enough water to quench your thirst. There in the darkness we endured the monotonous tread of a semi-life from which the only escape was death by starvation, death from illness or the nightmare of the living death, night and day. Living lost its meaning. Everything seemed the same. I remember crouching on the floor of the wagon wondering if I was alive or dead, feeling the pain of hunger churning in my stomach and chewing on the hem of my dress.

The train rattled on, further and further into the depths of the Soviet Union. We had finished most of our food. People were demented from lack of water. It had been weeks since we were confined to the wagons. No one slept for more than a few hours at a time except the people who were dying. The days and nights became one.

Now that we were on Soviet soil the soldiers seemed to be much more at ease. There were regular stops and the wagon doors were unbolted. Six or eight people would be summoned outside under armed guard. Everyone shrank back when the soldiers first unlocked the doors. We didn't know what would happen to those summoned to leave the wagon. But they returned unharmed, carrying buckets of snow — enough for everyone to have a handful. It was such a relief to plunge your filthy dirty face into a fistful of snow and to feel its coldness in the back of your throat.

The snow melted quickly in the close atmosphere of the wagon and for a few hours there was plenty to drink. It was a preoccupation, to crouch there and roll a lump of snow around in your mouth, revelling in the cold wet taste. But the relief was short-lived. The need for more food and water always occupied our minds. Mama hoarded what was left of our food, and every day she handed us a tiny lump of bread while no one was watching. There were people with no food left to eat. They were starving.

It seemed like a miracle when one day the train stopped and the soldiers called each family to the open door. They had a huge list with black crosses marking the names of people who had died. Those of us left were given a loaf of bread, one for each family. I remember staring at that bread. It was a small round loaf of hard black bread, and it made my mouth water.

Mama took the bread when our names were called. She held it reverently, as if it were a precious gift, then she tore it into five pieces. There was a small hunk each. The door rolled shut. The train jerked to a start. I stuffed the bread into my mouth, all of it at once, chewing with my mouth wide open. And then it was gone. It was not enough to stave off the hunger for very long, but it seemed to be a sign of hope. They were feeding us and so we knew we would not die yet.

It got colder and colder in the wagon. We seemed to be travelling north, deeper into the heart of the country. Now we were wearing all our clothes, layers and layers of dirty mismatched things dragged from the bundles we had packed in haste. The train stopped. We huddled together, shivering when the guards opened the door. No one wanted to go out and fill the buckets with snow. It was too cold. The snow was thigh high and there was no way to dry wet clothes in the wagon.

'Four people!' the guards shouted. 'Hurry up!'

No one wanted to go. Slowly, slowly, three men and a woman stepped down from the wagon. The wind howled outside. I crept to the door and looked out. There was nothing. Just vast stretches of snow as far as the eye could see. In front of the wagon the guard stared straight ahead with the hood of his *kulfika* tied tight.

Stumbling along in the snow at the side of the track, the four people from our wagon came back. This time they were carrying buckets of coal and a can of some sort of steaming liquid. They passed the buckets up into the wagon and climbed inside. The door was slammed shut.

'Here,' said one of the men who had left the wagon. 'A present from Father Stalin,' and he walked around the wagon filling people's mugs with the steaming liquid which he called soup. It didn't matter that the soup looked like murky brown water with pieces of hairy gristle floating on top. It was food, lukewarm and tasting vaguely of cabbage. We poured that soup down our throats as if it were the finest champagne.

With the food and the coal the mood in the wagon lightened for a while. Men lit the stove and people took turns to stand close, warming themselves. But the train clattered on. You could endure the meaningless existence if you were healthy, but for the sick every hour, every minute was torment and there was nothing to alleviate the suffering of people in pain. Every three or four days the soldiers would open the door and ask for dead bodies. There were no burials. A family would shuffle forwards with the body of a grandmother or perhaps a child and the soldiers would fling it outside on to the frozen ground. Two, three or four dead bodies would be piled out there, one on top of the other, and that was their grave.

It frightened me. Death was so very close. People were dying and no one could save them. I climbed up to the top *prycze* when it was my turn to have a rest. On the bottom lay a *babchia*. She reached out with her crow-like hand and grabbed my leg.

'*Dzien dobri*,' she said. When I climbed down she was dead. Stiff and still. Her daughter was crying and stroking her head. When the soldiers opened the wagon people dragged the old lady to the door. Her body was thrown outside. Its eyes were open wide. Her daughter threw herself after the body. She was shot in the head. There was no today and no tomorrow, just the noise of the wagon on the tracks and the long, long wait until the next piece of bread. Then when I thought I was going crazy the train stopped. Soldiers marched up and down alongside the wagons, banging on the walls. They slid open the door and shouted at us to come out. We were stiff and frightened, too scared to move. Only the bravest boys started to climb down. 'Move along … move …' the soldiers ordered, waving their guns.

For the first time since leaving Poland, we climbed out, walking like floppy straw dolls. I was a child. In Poland I had been running through the wheat fields, laughing and playing. Now I could hardly move my limbs. My body felt strange and disconnected. Outside there was nothing. Just snow. White blinding snow as far was you could see and the train with its trail of box wagons, carrying its human freight.

It was good to move your feet, to hold your head high and swing your arms. I gulped down huge breaths of the fresh cold air. In those few minutes the bitterness of life turned. My lifeblood soared and living felt full of promise. I smiled at Mama and she smiled back at me.

Shouting broke out behind us. We turned to look. Here in the middle of nowhere, without supplies of food, four or five men ran away. We saw them plunge like swimmers, diving into the snow, flailing their arms and legs, trying to run, trying to hide. Perhaps they thought they could outrun the bullets or perhaps it was sheer desperation at the thought of being shut back inside the wagons. Mama bent to pick up a handful of snow and pressed it up against her face. Marysia and I did the same.

'Don't look,' Auntie Danuta said. 'Cover your eyes.'

The soldiers fired into the snow. I did look. Pausing to get another handful of snow I saw them fire, faces staring straight ahead. In a second the snow was stained red. A deep crimson red. The men lay dying not more than two hundred metres from the wagon. The sound of the guns reverberated in my head. Sharp staccato shots. We pushed and fought to get back inside the dark recesses of that smelly cattle wagon. The soldiers locked the door. Women were screaming in high-pitched panicky voices. I was afraid. The death that haunted the wagon was so different from that violent red-coloured death outside.

Day and night the train rolled on. I stopped wondering about where we were going. I was no longer concerned about what would happen to us. My brother Feliks spent as much time as he could staring out the little window. 'Listen Kryska,' he said one day after climbing down the rope ladder. 'There are hundreds of us on this train. I have counted ninety people in our wagon and when the train goes around a corner I can count the wagons in front of and behind us. I know that there are a hundred and ten wagons. That makes nearly a thousand people.'

Feliks noted all these details in his diary. He reminded

me so much of Tata, the way he recorded facts and observations with intense concentration. Every day now the soldiers passed in a bucket of coal for the stove. One bucket, that was all. Standing close to the stove was now the most favoured position in the wagon. You could toast your face, your back and your sides until someone else pushed through to take their turn.

Perhaps we were getting closer to our destination. The train stopped for hours at a time. We could hear the wagons being uncoupled and the noise of engines as they were driven away. Then the train started up again with a great clanking and jerking, backwards and forwards and suddenly backwards again. I was glad that I was not warming myself. The people who were standing nearest the stove fell on to the hot metal, singeing their arms and their faces, burning their hands. The stink of burning flesh filled the wagon. People were screaming, their faces contorted with the pain.

It was the burning that seemed to tip the balance. Everyone was more unsettled. People were going crazy, shouting out all the time, calling for things that they wanted, dancing and singing as if they did not know where they were. It was odd to see grown-up people behaving in such strange ways. Some people took off all their clothes, men threw themselves again and again at the carriage walls. People tore their hair and pummelled their faces until the bruises shone bluish-green in the half-light.

It was a nightmare to be treated as less than human, to be locked up in a dark stinking wagon without enough water or food, with no idea of where we were going. To throw out the dead on to the frozen wastelands where the wolves would tear the bodies apart. That was a nightmare. And then the wagons stopped rolling. We braced ourselves, standing and waiting for the jolting as the train started moving again. This time there was nothing. Silence descended like a blanket of snow, but even before the quiet had settled people started pounding on the walls, begging the soldiers to open the doors. Others tried to stop them banging. The wagon was home to us now. No one knew what might be waiting outside.

The solders slid open the door and called us out. 'Hurry, hurry,' they shouted.

We climbed down, out of the wagon, not knowing whether we were going to live or die. We stood in the snow and waited, watching the thin dirty people who looked like ourselves climb out of the neighbouring carriages. There was not much to carry with us. We had eaten all the food and turned the sacks inside out to make sure that we'd found every dry dusty crumb.

The soldiers searched the wagon. They dragged out the old and the sick. They dragged out people who were dying and could not stand upright and left them lying in the snow, without anything to rest their heads on. An officer marched up to our wagon and began reading our names from a list. We were counted three or four times and were ordered into lines. Then the soldiers shouted, 'March, march,' and they ran alongside us with their guns banging against their thighs.

We were walking towards some sort of settlement. In

the distance I could see smoke rising. The soldiers seemed rough. They used the butts of their guns to hurry people along but we were all weak and stiff from being kept in the cattle wagons for so long, and within minutes our feet were soaking. Those who were stronger tried to help those who were falling behind. Both Mama and Auntie Danuta gave their arms to old women, trying to help them stay upright in the snow; Feliks gave his shoulder to an elderly man. I wished that there was someone who would take my arm, but I just kept on walking through the snow. People were falling over. The soldiers stood over the fallen bodies, kicking them, trying to make them stand upright again. We trailed on. The snow was quite deep in places, up to my knees.

I lifted my head and looked at the bedraggled procession of half-starved people around me. And then I saw it. There was a sign half buried in the snow.

'Mama, mama,' I shouted and struggled through the snow towards the sign. Perhaps I heard the blows coming. I don't know. My head was hurting. My face was bleeding and Feliks was dragging me along in the snow, holding me under the arms. My legs didn't seem to be working properly and Mama was walking beside me, crying. The column of Poles was still walking, walking, walking.

'What did it say, Mama?' I asked, even though I could hardly move my lips.

'Arhangel'sk,' Mama said.

'What does it mean?' It seemed important to make sense of the sign, even if all I wanted to do was lie down in the snow and rest my head.

'It means that we are in Siberia,' Feliks whispered. 'Now keep walking.'

I stopped thinking about my aching head. If this was Siberia, then I knew that we were going to die, because in Poland everyone knew of that vast frozen wasteland to which people were exiled with no return.

We walked and walked until we reached a large flat clearing in the snow. Here the soldiers called a halt. In front of us were a number of big flat wooden sledges. The soldiers got out their lists. They indicated that when your name was called you were to step on to one of the platform sledges. Mama, Marysia, Feliks and my names were called one after the other. We had to step out and leave Auntie Danuta behind. Soon there were at least a hundred people crowded on to the sledge. The soldiers drove tractors into the clearing and harnessed them to the sledges. With the roar of the tractor engines, the next journey began. We clung to each other as the sledge heaved over the snow drifts, heading in the direction of the forest.

It was beautiful in a way, being surrounded by tall green conifers which brushed the ground with their wide sweeping branches laden with snow. It was a relief to be outside breathing the fresh cold air. I forgot about my aching face and stared about me. Feliks and I touched our hands together in the secret signal that we still had from our childhood, palm to palm with our little fingers entwined. The tractors ground their way through the snow and soon the beauty of the forest faded as the cold tore at our bodies and hunger curled in our stomachs. My mouth was so dry.

I longed for a gulp of water, but now I knew that if you jumped off the sledge even to grab a handful of snow the soldiers would be swift and brutal.

The afternoon shadows lengthened and still the sledges drove on. The evening was short before the oncoming night but the soldiers drove on, lighting the way with the tractor headlights. It was late at night when the soldier driving the leading truck pulled into a clearing and the tractors ground to a halt. The officer who had been sitting all day in the cab of the truck stepped out into the headlights. The engines were turned off. Silence surged through the trees and the deep drifts of snow that banked the sides of the road. People shifted about uneasily on the sledges, wondering what would happen next. The officer cupped his hands around his mouth.

'Overnight stop,' he shouted in Russian. 'Bread and hot water will be issued.'

The soldiers pulled the men and boys off the sledges and sent them ploughing through the snowdrifts to gather firewood. They made huge piles of twigs and branches, doused them with petrol and set them alight. We climbed off the sledges and huddled around the fire. The flames lit the black night, sending up great dancing shadows against the backdrop of the trees. The soldiers leaned against the tractors, smoking cigarettes and watching as we tried to warm our hands and feet. It was like some strange picnic in the middle of nowhere, except that we had no food.

I scooped up huge handfuls of snow and pressed them into my mouth. The cold hurt my teeth but I could feel the ice melting to water and trickling down my throat. Mama was cleaning her face with snow; standing next to her was Auntie Danuta. She had climbed off one of the other sledges. I went to kiss her and she gasped at the sight of my face. I had forgotten about the bruises. They didn't seem to matter in this strange place where nothing made sense except hunger and cold. Feliks joined the firewood gatherers. You could hear them rustling around in the trees, wrenching huge boughs from the trunks by tearing and twisting. No one had an axe. The soldiers watched, not bothering to shout orders or stop people from wandering about. There was nowhere to hide, except in the forest where no one would stay alive for very long.

I stood, watching the flames, listening to Mama and Auntie Danuta talking about the best method of making sauerkraut. Marysia interrupted them. She was standing there with her hands deep in the pockets of her skirt.

'Mama,' Marysia said softly, 'where are we going to sleep?' Mama laughed. In the fresh cold air she seemed to have come alive. 'I don't know where we are going to sleep,' she said. 'Perhaps they think Poles are like horses and can sleep on their feet.'

As I listened to Mama and Marysia talking, the warmth from the fire seemed to lose its glow. I looked around at the people huddling together, shifting from one wet foot to the other, and knew that by the morning many would be dead. And I knew that our lives were of no account, just black crosses on a sheet of paper.

The soldiers set up camp on the other side of the fire

with the command truck and the supply truck parked side by side. The whole side of the supply truck swung open, revealing a small stove which the soldiers lit. Soon it was puffing out big clouds of smoke and the smell of food began wafting across the fire. We sniffed, noses to the air like a pack of hungry dogs.

Standing around on their side of the fire, the soldiers took turns eating from round tin plates. They didn't seem to see the faces staring ravenously at them. My mouth ran saliva and my stomach groaned aloud. I had to clench my fists to stop myself from running through the fire and begging those men to give us some food.

The darkness of the night closed in around us. There were wolves howling close by in the forest. The soldiers wiped their plates with pieces of bread. They lit cigarettes and lounged by the fire, laughing and talking. It seemed as if they were living in another world, one which we were forbidden to enter. I stared through the flames at the faces of those men, wondering if they had children who called them 'Father', wondering how they could laugh and talk while opposite them people were dying.

But they didn't let us starve. Some time towards the middle of the night the soldiers crossed to our side of the fire carrying cans of hot water and loaves of bread. It was heavy coarse black Russian bread. One small loaf for each family.

Mama grabbed our loaf and tore it into five even-sized pieces.

We stared at her hands. As she gave each of us a piece my mouth began dripping, and I couldn't stop myself stuffing it into my mouth. It was so good. I closed my eyes, swaying with pleasure, and felt the bread slipping down my throat. I tried to stop eating, to hold back from taking the next mouthful, but in less than a minute my bread was gone. I looked down at my hands in disbelief. My stomach was still growling but I had eaten everything. I took a sip from the can of hot water. Tears were running down my face. I desperately wanted another piece of bread.

Marysia was lucky. She seemed to have more self-control than me. She held her bread very close to her face and nibbled slowly around the edges until all that was left was a hard little lump. I watched her as she carefully folded the lump into her ragged sleeve. The cold of the night seemed to have deepened. I wished that I had managed to stop myself from gobbling up my whole piece of bread.

It was a long, long night. We stood in the snow and shivered.

It was so tempting to lie down in the soft white drifts, ignoring the cold and the wet. People took turns standing in front of the fire, toasting their faces, their backs and their freezing hands. Just as you felt the delicious warm thaw stealing across your body it was someone else's turn to stand by the fire and you shuffled backwards into the cold perimeter with soaking wet feet and hunger pawing the bottom of your stomach. People groaned aloud with the pain of keeping their bodies upright all night. The soldiers took turns sleeping in the trucks and on the sledges, wrapped in their padded *kulfikas*. Several times during the night we sniffed the tantalising aroma of their coffee.

It would have been a good time to escape but there was nowhere to run to. All around was the forest, the sighing of the trees and the howling of the wolves. People died in the night, lying on a bed of wet snow. As soon as the morning light filtered through the trees, relatives of the dead struggled into the forest and tore down branches. They covered the bodies with as many boughs as they could drag through the snow to try to protect the dead from the wolves.

The soldiers lit their stove and ate breakfast. We stood opposite them, watching and waiting. The fire had died down and no one had the energy to gather more wood. Soon the soldiers herded us into lines and back on to the platform sledges. This time Auntie Danuta managed to climb on to the same one as us. Her face was lined with fatigue but when she saw me watching her she smiled and put my hand deep into the pocket of her skirt. My fingers closed on a small hard lump of bread. I knew what it was as soon as I felt it. Every inch of my body tingled as I surreptitiously pulled that lump out of her pocket. Seconds later it was in my mouth.

I sucked that lump slowly, savouring the feel of food in my mouth. Auntie Danuta squeezed my hand and started singing a song from Poland. One by one the people around her picked up the tune, and after that mouthful of food it was easy for me to join in. The tractors started up and drowned out the noise of our singing, but somehow everyone felt a little cheered. We had survived another day of exile from our homeland. We had survived another day in the Soviet Union.

It was somewhere near the middle of the afternoon when the soldiers riding high on the back of the leading truck put away their playing cards. We all knew that something was about to happen. The soldiers pulled on their caps and boots and started running alongside the sledges, shouting at us.

On the sledges sleepers stirred. People had taken turns to lie between the legs and feet of those who were still standing. All day long our senses had been dulled by the swaying of the sledge, by our hunger and the intense cold. But now we were alert and looking around, wondering what was going to happen.

'Wherever we're going,' Auntie Danuta said to my mother, 'I think we are nearly there.'

We drove into a clearing in the forest and pulled up in a large open space in front of a wooden house. Stretching out behind us were several rows of newly constructed wooden buildings. The wood was so fresh that it oozed frozen sap down the walls. The soldiers began milling around, shouting orders. Everyone had to climb down and stand in a line with their bundles beside them. The soldiers seemed impatient, pushing and pulling, yanking Mama upright as she bent to tie together her bundle. I was scared. I stood stiff and still with my hands clenched together, closing my eyes when a soldier started hitting an elderly woman in front of me who could not stand by herself. The dull thud of blows hitting flesh made me feel sick to the bottom of my stomach. The camp commandant mounted a small stage in front of one of the buildings and immediately the soldiers stopped hitting and pushing. They stood to attention, clasping their guns at their sides. The commandant was a tall thin man with a greying beard and he seemed stern as he stood there looking down at us.

'You are interned here in Camp Niechodnik,' he said. 'The first rule is that those who do not work do not eat.'

We stood looking up at him with our stomachs raging with hunger. So there will be food, I thought to myself, and my heart beat wildly with anticipation. 'Work will be in the forest,' the commandant continued. 'You will provide logs for Father Stalin. You will be here until the hair grows on the palms of your hands. You will never return to the late Poland.'

I looked down at my hands. They were small and cold with smooth dirty palms. I knew that hairs would never grow on the palms of my hands. Beside me Mama, Marysia and Auntie Danuta were crying. I knew that we would be here forever.

Hard as it was, for a time life at the labour camp seemed to be an improvement on the conditions that we had endured during the train journey. It was cold, very cold, but at least we had somewhere to lie down at night and it was a space that became our own. Wood was easy to get. We were surrounded by forest and we made sure there was always a pile of freshly cut logs stacked by the stove. We slept on the floor, covering ourselves with the quilts we had brought from our home in Poland. During the night I would get up three or four times to drink water. For days I gulped great big handfuls of snow, trying to quench the thirst that was raging inside me. My lips were cracked and sore. I would eat snow and cry because I was so hungry. On our second day at the camp we started work. Everyone lined up outside and was allotted a work group. My job was in the timber yard where I had to feed logs into the splitting machine. My hours of work were until I had finished whatever daily quota the soldiers decided on. If I split enough wood I got half a kilogram of bread a day. It was black bread baked as hard as a brick and it came in lumps rather than slices.

My brother and sister went to work in the forest. They had to drag the felled timber to the river where it was floated south. They worked in gangs with five or six people chained to each side of the huge logs. Mama and Auntie Danuta worked at building roads. First they had to clear the stumps from the tracks, and from where I worked I could see groups of women tugging and heaving, up to their knees in sludge. They had no tools except metal chains for harnessing themselves to the stumps. Their quota was four stumps a day but sometimes it was all they could do to haul out one. Then their food quota was cut and the next day the women could hardly work because they were faint from starvation.

There was never enough to eat. As soon as the daily bread ration was eaten, your stomach was growling with hunger again. All day I fed wood into the chute and thought about food. I tried to eat chips of wood but they splintered my throat when I swallowed. We were paid a small amount of money for our work and sometimes the people who lived near the camp would bring things they wanted to sell. One day Mama bought some frost-bitten potatoes. She boiled them on the stove and we sat and waited with our eyes fixed on that can. There was a potato each. I cradled mine in my hand, savouring the warmth, and then I bit into it. The taste was vile, worse than the taste of rotten food, and I couldn't swallow. But before I could clear my mouth of that foul taste my mother was hitting me, holding her potato in one hand and hitting me with the other, shouting at me to eat my food. I swallowed that mouthful of frost-bitten potato, but I couldn't eat any more.

It seemed as if I was always frightened in the Siberian camp.

Wherever I went, whatever I did, I could feel a vicious overbearing harm lurking there, and nothing could take that evil presence from my mind. I wanted to be safe, to be as close as possible to my mother who was always so sad and tired. In the evenings, after work, I would hide away in dark corners. Any place where no one would find me. I would watch, wait and listen. Every night people died and in the morning those who were still alive piled the dead bodies outside the door of the barracks. The bodies were quite stiff. They looked like boards stacked one on top of the other. There were big lice everywhere, biting your body and crawling around in your hair, but as soon as a person died the lice left. All around us people were going mad. Sometimes they didn't work and then they had nothing to eat. Some people sat on the floor of the barracks for days, just sitting there until they stopped living. Others shouted and raged in their sleep. In the morning they went out to work in the forest but they were so tired they could not fulfil the work quota and so they got no food. There were always people crying and people dying. One morning everyone was shouting, 'Wariat, Wariat.' Right beside the camp there was a very swift river full of muddy water which swirled around the banks. We ran outside and there was a man standing in the middle of the river pulling up huge chains from under the water and tearing them apart with his hands. We stood on the bank watching. People were saying, 'Look how strong the mad man is.' I cowered in a corner behind the barracks and watched from a long way off. I was too scared to come any closer, and yet in a way I was fascinated and couldn't help staring at the mad man. Everyone was shouting and pointing; even the soldiers came to look at what was happening. Then the man lost his footing and fell into the water. His head disappeared and everyone walked off. I suppose he drowned. It was hard to live in this place where you were always hungry, always looking for food, where you were always frightened and nothing made sense any more.

# Chapter 4

I will always remember the Siberian spring. The air was soft and warm on my face. The strong clear daylight lasted so much longer, stretching into the late afternoon. There was a quickening of life about the camp. Each day seemed to be worth living. Fewer people died. Even the old and the sick managed to lift up their heads and look into the sun.

There was a flurry of activity around the barracks. Women came back from working in the forest with bundles of twigs under their arms. They swept out every corner of the wooden buildings and then turned their attention to themselves. Steam rose from the tins piled on the stove as they boiled up washing water. Then the men were sent outside while the women and children stripped themselves bare. I remember staring down at my body. It looked so different from the body I'd had on bath days in Poland. I was taller and thinner with a thick layer of dirt covering my arms, legs and feet. We used handfuls of pine needles to scrub ourselves and washed what was left of our clothes. While they were drying we washed our hair. There was no soap so you could not make yourself really clean, but we wet our hair in the boiled water and rinsed it with melted snow. Then we wrapped ourselves in our bedding and sat together picking out lice from each other's hair and stamping them into the ground.

Some women said that the best way to get rid of lice was to comb petrol through your hair, but we had no petrol. Most of us didn't even have a comb. We made do with our fingers and bits of branches. No one cared what we looked like as long as we could continue to work. Sometimes in the evenings I would go for a walk past the commandant's house. Once I sniffed the pungent aroma of petrol and saw the commandant's wife sitting on the verandah combing it through her long dark hair. She looked to me like a princess out of a fairy story, except that somehow it was all wrong and the magic fairyland had changed into these ugly rows of wooden barracks and the dream was to get enough bread to stop your stomach growling.

I often disappeared into my imaginary world. I would close my eyes and see a girl in a pretty white dress with food all around her. Piles of bread and plates of potatoes. I could eat as much as I wanted and there was always more. People were kind and smiling. I could go and play in the forest without fear. No one was dying. But when I opened my eyes and looked around me, tears would come and the hunger would be raging inside my body, begging me to find it something to eat.

The short Siberian summer followed the beautiful spring.

Grasses and berries grew in the forest clearings and the days were so warm that you could walk outside without shivering. People who had brought seeds from Poland planted little gardens behind the barracks. Mama planted some onion seeds which she bought from one of the soldiers. She paid for the seeds with one of our heavy silver candlesticks.

Some days the sun shone. Beautiful rays of glowing light filtered through the trees and were warm on your face. It was like the memory I had of my warm bed in our house in Poland. The sun brought us life. The summer also brought us food in the forest. *Poziomki* and blackcurrants. *Lebiata* with its thick coarse green leaves. We ate everything that looked edible. Mama even boiled up potfuls of the fine green grass that appeared under the trees, but it gave us terrible stomach cramps. An old Polish woman scolded Mama. 'Only animals eat grass, Pani,' she said. 'Your children need bread.' At night we made jam. Mama boiled the blackcurrants in the pot that I remembered always being on the stove at home. There was no sugar for Mama's jam, so she just boiled the black currants until they made a thick paste. I found it reassuring to stand beside the stove, taking a turn to stir the fruit when Mama's arm got tired. She was so fatigued that she didn't speak to me. She just handed over the piece of wood when it was my turn to stir. I loved standing near her. I liked to watch her eyes narrow in concentration as she peered through the steam down into the pot. She did not comfort me but she was there, always trying to do things to make life a little easier for us. I could not imagine living without her.

Summer passed quickly and then came the autumn. Hundreds of mushrooms sprouted under the trees. We gathered them in our skirts, holding the edges together, and made huge, earthy-smelling mounds on the floor. At night we spread them out by the stove so that they would dry. Auntie Danuta threaded some on pieces of string and hung them from the rafters. It made the long wooden room seem more like home, and at night I would lie on the floor and gaze up at the strings of mushrooms, trying to count how many there were. Before I got to three hundred I fell asleep.

It was during the autumn that the baby was born. Every day I worried about my sister Marysia. She was always sick and always tired. Every morning she dragged herself out to the forest to work and returned in the evening staggering with fatigue. Sometimes Mama gave Marysia half of her bread ration. I always felt jealous and wondered why Mama didn't share her bread with me. I had no idea about the baby that was coming. It happened all of a sudden. I woke up in the night and saw Mama and Danuta kneeling by Marysia who was groaning loudly and tossing about. She seemed to be having some sort of violent fever. I got up and hid in the corner, wondering what was happening, why Mama was kneeling in front of her, looking up between her legs. Strange guttural noises were coming from Marysia's mouth. Auntie Danuta was helping her to turn over, and then Marysia was on her hands and knees with blood and stuff coming out of her. I wanted to scream but I stuffed my hands into my mouth and stared into the darkness, anxious and helpless. Then I heard a small thin cry and in the morning there was a tiny baby lying in a suitcase on the floor beside Marysia. I crept over to look at the small wrinkled-up face. The baby was wrapped in one of Mama's dresses and crying all the time. A thin high wailing sound. I looked over at Marysia but her eyes were closed. I wondered if she was all right. There was sweat running down her face. Mama sent me to the commandant's house to ask for food for the baby. His wife came to the door and listened to my request. She sighed and wrinkled up her nose.

'Wait,' she said in Russian. After a while she came back with a bowl of porridge and a bundle of woollen clothes. 'Come back every morning at six,' she said. 'I will give you some food for the baby.'

I carried the bowl of porridge back to the barracks. It smelt so good that I tried to hold it as far as I could from my face. But I was hungry, so very hungry that I had to dip my finger into it. Two, three or four times I dipped in my finger and sucked up the gruel. I felt so guilty eating the baby's porridge but I couldn't stop. It was my stomach which was telling me what to do.

Mama grabbed the porridge from my hands as soon as

I came through the door of the barracks. She mixed it with water, soaked the corner of a rag and pushed it in between Marysia's lips. She was too ill to suck the cloth. Mama tried to get the baby to suck on the rag. I went outside to work. I couldn't bear to see Mama trying to feed that watery gruel to Marysia and the baby when she should have been eating it herself. Mama didn't go to work that day, and when I came back from the timber yard Marysia had died. She was still lying there on the floor but there was blood all over the rags that covered her. Mama said that she had bled to death. I wondered why and I hated that baby that had come out of her and was lying there in Mama's arms crying so loudly. I washed my dead sister's face and tried to comb her hair with my fingers. When Auntie Danuta came back from work we carried the body outside. There was a huge pit behind the barracks where the guards threw the dead bodies. I wanted Marysia to have her own grave but the ground was hard and there was nothing I could use for digging. Danuta and I climbed down into the pit and put Marysia's body on top of the others. Tears were pouring down my face, choking me. I thought that I would cry forever. People died every day in this place, but now death had taken someone in my family. I felt lonely and frightened without Marysia. I wondered who would die next.

The summer passed quickly and soon it was winter again. The feeling of liveliness faded. People walked around slowly with their heads covered and their arms wrapped tightly around their bodies, trying to keep in some warmth. They looked like old scarecrows with threadbare clothes and bundles of rags around their feet. Our shoes had worn out months ago and we improvised with layers of bark and strips of rag. At night we would unwrap our feet and put the rags by the stove to dry, but in the morning they were still damp and felt clammy as you bound them around your legs. It was like a premonition of the day to come. Wet hands, wet head, wet feet, water trickling down your back and the heavy damp smell of perspiration as you tried to keep up with the work quota.

Every morning I went to the commandant's wife to get porridge for the baby. We called him Maciek and Mama baptised him herself. Every time I looked at him tears sprang to my eyes and I thought of poor Marysia. During the day Mama and Danuta took the suitcase to a room at the end of the barracks where a woman looked after five or six tiny children who were too young to work. Baby Maciek seemed to be getting thinner and thinner. He did not eat his porridge and Mama gave it to me. He lay asleep in his suitcase cradle and his skin was like an old man's, all papery and grey. I didn't ever pick him up and hold him, but every day I looked to see if he was still alive. I didn't cry when he died. The commandant's wife gave Mama a white cloth to wrap around the little body.

Life became very grey. Nothing seemed to change. We worked and ate our daily ration of bread. We slept. Every day people got sick and died. Slowly life began to fade before my eyes and I could hardly see. In the mornings my eyes opened as usual but all I could make out were vague shapes. I hesitated about telling Mama, as she was always worrying;

instead I crept around, feeling my way, peering through eyes that didn't seem to focus any more. Then, one morning as I was rubbing my eyes, trying to see better, Feliks said quietly, 'I can't see.' It was such a relief to hear him say it. Then Auntie Danuta confessed that she was having trouble with her eyes, and I told them about mine.

It wasn't only our family that was affected. Everyone was talking about the night blindness, and an elderly doctor who had been deported with us said that it was starvation that was making us blind. No one listened to the old man. They told him to be quiet. The fact that our blindness was caused by lack of food made people uneasy because you simply couldn't get more food, even if you had money. In winter the Russians who lived near the camp had nothing to sell and the soldiers would trade things only for onion seed.

The blindness worsened. People went out to work in the forest and never came back. Once evening fell they were unable to see where they were going and had no idea of the direction of our barracks. Everyone felt powerless to do anything about the blindness except Bronislaw Suchocki. Feliks said that he had been a lawyer in Poland, and in the labour camp he was always making representations to the commandant to try to improve things for us. Bronislaw had already spent two weeks in the prison under the commandant's house because he had asked for a bread ration for the men and women who were too old to work in the forest. Now Bronislaw talked to many of the people who were going blind. He made notes about the seriousness of their condition, and one night he walked to the commandant's house and knocked at the door.

We were sure we would never see him again. To the commandant we were just nameless Poles, sentenced to a lifetime of labour in the forests. Our living conditions were unimportant. Those who died were replaced in the work gangs by newcomers from another transport. The commandant would not listen to Bronislaw, we said, and he would be punished for his impudence. We could hardly believe it when he turned up later that night, alone and unharmed. 'The commandant will help us,' Bronislaw said. 'If we cannot see, then we cannot work. This time it is an issue of work, not bread.'

Weeks later, several barrels of cod-liver oil arrived and everyone had to line up for a spoonful a day. It tasted thick and fishy but in two weeks my eyes were better and I could see at night again. The commandant always attended the cod-liver oil assembly and lectured us about the kindness of Father Stalin.

The cold, the hunger and our dim prospects for the future depressed our spirits as did the fact that the commandant used to take people away for interrogation during the night. When the soldiers came for Mama, Feliks and I were terrified. All night we sat awake, praying that our mother would be returned to us. I was so tired, my tongue kept tripping over the words, but I knew that Mama would not be sleeping and I was determined to stay awake and keep her company. Just before the work detachments left for the forest, Mama returned to the barracks. She was very pale and her eyes seemed to have sunk deep into her head. Without a word she joined her gang and plodded down the track to pull out more stumps. Without work there was no bread.

Every week more and more people died. Faces that had become familiar were suddenly not there any more. The hunger dragged you down. Every day I went to look at the onions that Mama had planted. They were growing in rows with thick green stems, and suddenly I couldn't stand just looking at them any more. I dragged three or four of them out of the ground and gobbled them up. The taste was strong but not unpleasant, and then they hit my stomach. The pain was agonising, a terrible burning sensation. I curled up into a tight ball and bit my lips, trying not to cry out. It would have been better to stay hungry than to eat those onions, but the need to eat tormented me. Sometimes I wished that I was dead. If hunger plagued us during the long days, at night things were worse. People lay on the floor crying out in their sleep, twitching and sobbing. Men were crying too. Often they were calling out for something they had left behind or for a little thing that they had treasured. Others would call for an egg or a piece of cake. It made me very sad to hear all those people with sad thin faces crying for what they could not have.

Day and night, life dragged on. It was a long slow life in death. We were not beaten or tortured but we were starved. Death was the only alternative to this grey half-life. Mama and Danuta scarcely spoke. They dragged themselves around with their shoulders hunched and their heads bowed. At night Mama sat on the floor by the stove, rocking herself from side to side. Sometimes I sat beside her but she never spoke to me. She just sat there muttering to herself, rocking backwards and forwards with an incessant motion.

Ever since I was taken from my home as a child, I have felt lonely for the warmth of a loving smile, for a mother's kiss or an arm around my shoulder. I wished that someone would stretch out their arms and take me away from this deep loneliness, take me away to a place where the sun shone and there was plenty of bread.

As our strength ebbed there were terrible accidents in the Siberian forest. Every two or three days someone would crawl back to the barracks with a broken limb or a torn hand. There was nothing to ease the pain. They either lived or died. Life promised them nothing in return and death was often a welcome call.

I was working in the timber yard when they carried Feliks in from the forest. His right leg was smashed and there were pieces of bone sticking up through the skin. The soldiers put him down on the floor and I ran to him. His eyes were closed but I leaned on his chest and listened to his heart. It was beating softly. I was so relieved that he was not dead.

There was no one to help me. The old doctor had died. Mama was working out in the forest and had been on half rations for two weeks. She was so tired and thin that she could scarcely walk. Soon she would be too feeble to work and then there would be even less food to eat. I boiled some water, all the time talking away to myself, trying to work out what to do. Feliks lay on the floor, pale and still. People started coming in from work and as they went past some of them suggested things I could do to ease Feliks's pain. Someone put some willow-bark strips in the boiling water. All around me people were talking, sighing when they looked down at my brother's leg. I bathed the bloody mess of a leg, trying not to look at the bright blood oozing from the wound. There was a sharp piece of bone sticking sideways through the flesh. I pushed down on it, pressing hard. Feliks screamed in pain and women around us held him down, telling me to push harder, to try to put that piece of bone back in place. I didn't know how to do it but I tried to push the bone flat and then bound the leg. Someone passed me a pile of birch bark and I tore strips from my dress to use as bandage. The women who had held Feliks walked away. Accidents were an everyday occurrence, merging life with death. I wished that there was someone to help me, to take away Feliks's pain, to give us bread.

I sat beside Feliks, checking for the ebb and flow of his breath. I bathed his head with warm water and trickled drops in between his lips. There was nothing else I could do except wait for him to live or die. And then Mama came, breathless from hurrying. She pushed past me and grabbed Feliks's body, holding him close and sobbing.

'Please Mama,' I said softly. 'Let him lie down.'

But she would not let Feliks out of her arms. She was crying so loudly and with such abandon that even in this place people stared at her.

'Feliks, my little one,' she cried, kissing his forehead and trying to put his arms around her neck.

I tried to get Mama's attention but she shook me aside. I felt so helpless because I knew that Feliks was unconscious with pain and that his body needed to rest. From somewhere a woman came over to help me. I didn't know who she was but she put her arm around Mama's shoulder and quietly led her away to sit by the stove. I sat down beside Feliks and bathed his head.

It seemed like hours before Auntie Danuta came. She had worked in the forest until after dark, trying to finish her work quota. Even though she was shaking with fatigue she gave me some of her bread, crumbling it into a paste with water, and showed me how to spoon it between Feliks's lips so that he would not choke.

All night I sat awake beside my brother. I held his hand and talked to him. I sang him Polish songs. Sometimes I was not sure whether he was alive or dead so I lay with my head on his chest, listening for the beating of his heart. In the morning I went and asked to be transferred from the timber yard to the latrines. The soldiers stared at me, but then put my name on the latrine list. No one wanted the job of cleaning the toilet pits, but I knew that there I would be much closer to the barracks and would be able to look after Feliks as well as keep up with the work.

Every morning I cleaned his wounded leg with boiling water and made a new plaster of birch bark, which Auntie Danuta brought in from the forest. There was not much else she could do to help. Mama sat quietly beside Feliks in the evenings but she did not speak at all. She moved around like someone in a daze.

All day I carried buckets of shit to the open pits. The stink was terrible and the buckets were very heavy. I had to walk quite slowly so that the shit didn't splash on to the rags which I bound around my legs. Every day, though, Feliks got a little better. I watched him so closely that I could tell from the twist of his lips how much pain he was suffering. His leg was purple and swollen, but the infection seemed to be contained. I knew that if it spread he would die. We had nothing to stop the infection, nothing but hope.

It seemed as if I was always plunging my arms into a can of boiling water, scrubbing my hands of the dirt from the latrines, but I was so afraid of bringing infection to Feliks and I had to touch him. Some days he sort of smiled at me as I bathed his leg. That was a good day. There were other days when he writhed and twisted about, shouting for his gun. If Mama was there she would shout back at him, telling him to go away and leave us in peace. Then I worried that he would hear her and die.

In some ways it was good having Feliks to care for. It took my mind away from the raging emptiness of my stomach. I tried to find ways of making life more bearable for him, and while I worked I looked for things to show him. A stone or a leaf, a lump of snow to wet his dry lips. After a while I didn't really notice the stench from the buckets and I never looked down into the pits. I did the work as fast as I could so that I could get back to my brother.

One day I was walking across the compound with a

bucketful of shit in each hand, when a Russian soldier shouted out, 'You, come here!'

I was scared of the soldiers. They were rough and brutal. I had seen them beat up an old lady who wouldn't let go of her dead husband's body. In the end they threw her into the dead people's pit with him. I was scared but I knew that you had to obey their orders, so I put my buckets down and went over to the guard. He reached inside his coat and gave me a newspaper.

'Here,' he said, 'you Poles are free,' and he gave me a little push backwards in the direction of my buckets.

I dumped the shit and ran straight to Feliks. He was lying as usual with his eyes closed. 'Look … look …' I said excitedly. 'It says here that we are free to go,' and I started reading the newspaper to him in Russian.

Feliks opened his eyes and looked straight at me. 'Is this a trick?' he asked. 'A trick to make me feel better?'

I laughed and cried, smothering his head with kisses. Then I showed him the newspaper and explained how a soldier had given it to me. Together we read and re-read the words in Russian. It was a long time since we had heard anything about the war. Occasionally someone would surreptitiously hand on a tiny scrap of paper which had been folded and re-folded many times. We would read the words and memorise them before handing it on to someone else. But this time the news was different. The newspaper said that Hitler had attacked the Soviet Union which in turn had become one of the Allied Powers. A Polish-Soviet Pact had been signed in July 1941 which granted an amnesty to all Polish citizens who were imprisoned in the Soviet Union. The agreement also provided for the raising of a Polish army under Polish command on Soviet territory.

Feliks and I read the news again and again. His eyes were bright. 'Listen, Krystyna,' he said, 'you had better run out into the forest and tell the work gangs the news.'

'But why?' I asked him. 'We can tell them tonight. I don't want to go out there in the forest.' A warning was sounding in my head. I didn't want to do anything that would attract attention to myself.

'Please go ... for me,' Feliks whispered softly. 'They have no hope out there ... you will bring them the good news.'

I stuffed the newspaper into the waistband of my skirt and ran. Out the door and down the track, out into the forest. I didn't worry about the guards seeing me. Even if I was planning to escape there was nowhere to run to and I had no food to help me survive. My feet were wet and heavy but I ran and ran. My boots had worn out several months ago and now the rags that I had bound around my feet became loose. I shook them off and kept running, heading for the clearing where the main forest gang was working. Piotr Rybacz was working there stacking logs. I ran into the clearing and launched into my tirade, shouting the news without pausing for a breath.

Piotr leaned against a stack of logs, listening. I could see that he didn't believe me so I hauled out the newspaper from my skirt and waved it under his nose. He took it and questioned me closely, asking who had given me the newspaper and who had sent me out into the forest. Then he read the news slowly as it was in Russian. He looked at me, and then read it again. Suddenly he grabbed me and shouted, '*Amnastia!*' at the top of his voice, throwing me up in the air and catching me in his arms. '*Amnastia! Amnastia!*' he shouted over and over in his deep booming voice.

People emerged from the forest like thin silent shadows. They stood around in the clearing, shifting from one foot to the other. Their faces were ravaged and gaunt. There were many children among them. Their parents were too ill to fulfil the work quota and the children went to work in the forest in their place. When the clearing was full of silent forest workers Piotr lifted me up on top of a stack of wood.

'Speak,' he ordered, 'shout as loudly as you can.'

Once again I recited the facts and waved the newspaper. My voice seemed to be hoarse and trembly. No one moved. They stood there staring at me as I spoke, their eyes dulled by cold and hunger. I started climbing down from the woodpile and slowly the noise began. A thin ragged cheer that gradually gained in force until everyone was singing. Arms lifted me down. People hugged and kissed me. I was passed from arm to arm, from hand to hand. Women were kneeling on the snow thanking God for their deliverance. Men were crying and hugging each other. Their trousers were in tatters and they had no boots, but now there was hope, a thin sliver of hope that we might be saved from death in this cold hungry place.

On the amnesty day no one completed their work quota. Everyone was talking, making plans to leave this place. They lit huge bonfires out there in the forest and stood around warming themselves. Piotr boiled up cans of water and we took turns to drink a toast to Poland and our return home. In the evening everyone marched back to camp singing and praying. Change was in the air.

The commandant was standing in the camp square. The soldiers were in rows beside him, standing at attention. Our singing died. Orders were given for us to form lines. The guards were especially rough, hustling those who were slow at getting into place. But there was a different sort of feeling among us. People moved around more quickly, trying to avoid the soldiers. They stood with their heads up, looking ahead instead of staring down at the mushy snow on the ground.

The commandant mounted his platform and stared down at us. Everyone stood silent and still, waiting for him to speak. 'Poles,' he said, 'I have not received any official information about this so-called amnesty. Work will continue as usual.'

The crowd was no longer a subdued throng of scarecrows. They muttered to themselves and jostled about, waiting impatiently for the commandant to finish talking.

'I will not tolerate any dissidence in this camp,' the commandant shouted. 'Krystyna and Feliks Wishnowski will be imprisoned for twenty-one days.'

That was my name, I thought — and then two guards grabbed me by the elbows. Auntie Danuta screamed out and tried to grab hold of me; the guards kicked her sideways. Holding my arms tight they dragged me along between them. I wriggled and fought, biting and scratching like a wild cat, trying to get away from them.

'Quiet!' one of the soldiers snapped, twisting my arm until it felt as if it was breaking. People were staring as the soldiers dragged me along. I shouted, '*Amnastia, amnastia*' ... as loudly as I could. The cry spread and soon everyone was shouting, '*Amnastia!*' raising their skinny arms and shouting at the tops of their voices.

The guards shoved a rag in my mouth. It tasted foul and I could hardly breathe. They marched me towards the cellar prison underneath the commandant's house. I wriggled and fought but they were too strong. They opened the door, threw me inside face first, and bolted the door. It was dark and the ground felt wet. I huddled where I had fallen, feeling the black dampness close in around me. In the depths of the darkness I heard a sort of shuffling. Something was moving.

'A rat!' I screamed and screamed, throwing myself against the door and scrabbling madly against it. But the door was securely bolted. There was no way out. Then I heard the scuffling noise again. It was too big for a rat. Terrified, I peered into the darkness. Feliks, my darling brother Feliks, was trying to drag himself across the ground towards me.

'Kryska,' he whispered, 'come over here, little one.' I crawled over to him. The cellar roof was so low that you could not stand upright. 'We will be all right,' he said, propping himself on an elbow so that he could stroke my head.

'But what about your leg?' I asked him.

'Hush … don't worry.'

We lay together on the cold wet ground. I talked and sang.

Feliks seemed to sleep most of the time. I was hungry, terribly, terribly hungry. We had missed our evening slice of bread and there was nothing to drink. In the darkness hunger seemed like a huge demon waiting to engulf us. I was afraid that we would die in this dark damp cellar and that no one would care.

As soon as Feliks was awake I asked him if he thought we would get out alive. 'Of course,' he reassured me. 'As soon as they get official notification of the amnesty they will have to let us out.'

'Maybe they won't,' I said, weeping again.

Feliks tried to make me forget my fears by asking for stories, and soon I was remembering our home in Poland and all the animals. Perhaps that's why I didn't notice how sick he was. After three or four days Feliks was delirious. His leg had swollen around the badly set bone and his clothes were wet with perspiration. He talked in his sleep, raving about Mama and Tata, talking tenderly to Marysia even though she was dead. I tried to keep myself going with prayers and songs. Sometimes I would hear someone walking overhead in the commandant's house and then I crouched on the ground and pounded on the floor above us, begging and pleading for someone to let us out of that dreadful place. Once the door opened and light poured in. A soldier put a can of water on the ground, together with a small loaf of bread. I grabbed the can of water and carefully crawled back to Feliks, trying not to spill a drop. I raised his head and poured some water in between his lips. He coughed and swallowed. I fed him a few more drops of water and then I seized the bread and tore off a huge chunk, chewed it and swallowed. I tried to put a piece between Feliks's lips but he was too ill to eat it. I chewed the bread for him, scooping it out of my mouth and pressing it in between his lips. If I gave him a sip of water he could swallow most of the pulpy mess.

We ate the bread slowly. I would have a mouthful and then chew one for Feliks. The bites got smaller and smaller and then the bread was finished. There was nothing left. Nothing. Feliks was still and silent. We lay there together while I talked to him about Poland, about summer, about anything at all that came into my head. Maybe I spoke nonsense. I don't know. Feliks was silent. He didn't answer any of my questions. I lay with my head on his shoulder, talking myself inside out.

Then at last they opened the door. A crack of light spread itself wider and wider through the cellar and a hoarse man's voice ordered us to come out. I couldn't move. My legs didn't work any more. My eyes were blinded by the light. And then I heard Polish voices. It was like being in heaven. Arms lifted me up and carried me out of the damp darkness into the light. When they brought Feliks out he was dead.

I was sick for a long time. I could not eat or drink. Every

time I shut my eyes I was back there in the cellar with Feliks beside me. I did not know my mother or my aunt. I just lay there on the floor of the barracks and my body ceased to function. Sometimes I woke from a deep drifting sleep and heard voices. Polish voices. They were talking about leaving the camp and making a journey south. Sometimes there were people trying to feed me bread mixed with water. They forced it into my mouth even though I tossed my head away from the spoon. The taste of that bread paste reminded me of Feliks. I wanted him to be alive. I didn't deserve to live if he had died with my head on his shoulder.

I think it was Auntie Danuta who helped me to come back to life. One day when I woke she was lying on the floor beside me. There was a huge gash in her arm where she was hit by a spade after intervening in a fight. Her arm had swelled to three or four times its size. She could not work and we lay side by side on the floor, gathering strength.

She talked to me all the time, about Poland and the animals, the flowers and our farm. She held me with her good arm and stroked my head. I opened my eyes to see her poor tired face looking lovingly at me. She smiled and kissed my head. After a few days I was able to get up and bathe her arm in warm water. As I came to my senses I noticed that things had changed. People were busying themselves, tying and re-tying their small bundles.

'We are going to leave this place,' Auntie Danuta told me. 'The commandant has received official notification of the amnesty for all Poles. We are free to leave here if we wish.'

You could see that no one in the camp was planning to stay. Even the old and ill were getting themselves ready to leave. No one had much to take with them. Some people raised a little bit of money by selling the last things they owned. Our family had nothing to sell, no food, no spare clothes and no decent footwear for the journey, but I knew that these things would not deter Mama. No one wanted to spend another winter in Siberia where life was just a postponement of death by starvation.

People were ready to leave. They knew that in this season the road south was passable and that a hundred and twenty miles away there was a railway station. In small groups those who had survived the labour camp walked free. We went too, Mama, Danuta and me. My aunt could not carry anything because of her painful arm and I was still shaky from weeks of illness, but we both knew that it was important to get moving. I carried a half-empty black suitcase. Mama had a bundle and a pot on her back. We walked down the snow-covered road which was flanked on either side by the green birch forest. Our feet were wet and our stomachs were growling with hunger. In front and behind us tramped the tide of people leaving Arhangel'sk. Some were carrying their children and supporting their *babchias*. Others limped and stumbled along alone, mumbling prayers and curses to themselves. We all knew that whoever was left behind would never see Poland again.

We walked and walked down the road until we reached the nearest village, where Mama and I begged for food. It was easier than I thought it would be to knock on the doors of the small houses and ask for some bread in halting Russian. The local women seemed kind. They didn't have much food themselves but many of them gave us a few crusts of bread and a handful of wheat. They were astonished that we were leaving this God-forsaken place, as no one imprisoned in Arhangel'sk had ever been freed before.

We walked on and on along the railway line towards Kotlas. At night Mama and Danuta begged shelter in the villages. Mama had saved a strip of carefully folded lace, a square of which would buy us a night's rest in with the animals. In the mornings we re-wrapped the rags around our feet and kept on walking. I asked Mama where we were going but she said she didn't know. It was important for me to have some sort of direction in my head so I walked alongside Danuta, asking her to tell me where we were walking to.

'We are going to the railway station,' she said. 'We will get on a train and travel south, as far from this place as we can.' I felt better knowing what would happen next, but it was hard to walk all day when I was so hungry.

One night when it was snowing, a village woman let us come inside her house and sit on the high ledge behind the stove. Mama and Danuta went out begging for bread, but this time I was glad just to sit there and soak up the feeling of being warm and sheltered. The woman was baking bread, and the rich pungent smell of dough filled the room. I longed to eat. Every inch of my body craved food. The woman took the bread from the oven, put it on the table to cool and left the room. I watched from behind the stove. It was only for a moment, but there was just enough time for me to grab a hunk from the freshly baked loaf and cram it in my mouth. There wasn't time to chew and swallow, I just gulped it down and rushed back to my seat behind the stove. The woman came back and looked at the bread. I stared straight ahead, conscious only of the whirling sensation in my body and the relief of being able to put something in my belly.

I sat, waiting. After a while Mama and Danuta returned. Mama was very pale and tired. On this long walk she never seemed to notice me. She never mentioned my name or touched my shoulder. She just trudged on and on, with her eyes fixed on some distant point far in front of us. Now she crept into that village woman's house, cradling a few crusts of bread as if they were gold.

She had just started to unwrap the sodden rags from around her feet when the woman called to her. Mama climbed down from the ledge, and the woman began talking, pointing at me all the time. I just sat there, with my heart beating wildly in dread. The woman was so angry. 'Thief, thief ... ' she kept saying and pointing to me.

Mama gave the begged crusts to Danuta. Then she grabbed my arm and dragged me outside. I held back, trying to get away from her, but she was too strong. Then, outside the door of the village woman's house, she started beating me. Hitting and kicking. It hurt so much, on my head, my back, my neck and my stomach. I begged and screamed for her to stop while she clawed and scratched my face. My body hurt so much that I thought I was going to die, but I remember thinking that it was a good way to die because

Mama was right. It was wrong to steal that bread and now I would die for it.

I didn't die. We walked on and on. My body was sore. My face was puffy and swollen. Mama never looked my way. She did not speak to me at all. I begged for my own bread. When there was enough I tried to share it with Mama and Danuta. Mama would not take my bread even though she must have been hungry. Sometimes she tripped and fell down in the snow. Danuta and I would take hold of her arms and heave her back upright. That was the only time I came close enough to Mama to touch her.

We walked until we got to the railway station at Kotlas. All of a sudden the roads were crowded with Poles. People were everywhere, dragging themselves along. They all looked thin and dirty and were dressed in rags. There were bodies dead by the side of the road. It became harder to beg for food. I had to steal but I didn't tell anyone where the food came from. No one asked. Even Mama ate what I brought. I stared at her eating the stolen food and wondered why she hit me so hard when I took bread from the village woman. Nothing made sense to me any more. As soon as we had eaten the food I started looking for more.

In the middle of this hunger and sickness things were happening. People were organising a train to travel south and trying to get some money to pay our way. I saw the wedding rings go from Mama's and Danuta's thin fingers. They had nothing else left to sell. People were turning their rags inside out, trying to find something that would bring in a little bit of money. Every day I begged from door to door. '*Procze, Pani* … a little bread … ' but the Russian women said they had nothing to give and shut the door in my face. I took what I could. Bread, grain and, once, an egg. I fed the egg to my Aunt Danuta. Her silent lips sucked out the goodness and then she ate the shell.

Once again there were cattle wagons lined up at the station. This time we climbed inside without any prompting from the Soviet guards. We were travelling south to Tashkent where the Polish army was re-forming. There were promises of food and shelter there.

When we climbed up into the wagon it was already crowded. Sick and dying people were lying everywhere on the floor. They had sores on their arms and their faces. Everyone was thin and dirty. More and more people climbed in. Everyone had to go. No one wanted to be left there at the station. The wagon door was slid shut, but this time it was not locked on the outside. These things made no difference to us now. All we wanted to do was to get away.

We stood together in that wagon, trying not to take up too much space, lurching against each other whenever the train went around a corner. As we travelled south the air grew warmer and inside the wagon it was hot and fetid. Fevers spread. People were too sick to drag themselves to the toilet hole. I watched the life ebb out of those around me and wondered if I would be next.

## Chapter 5

I will always remember being on that train, suspended between life and death. It was only the growling and twisting of my stomach that told me I was alive. Sometimes the train slowed at a station; as soon as it stopped I'd be waiting at the door, ready to begin the search for food. No one knew how long the train would stop for — sometimes it was a few minutes, sometimes it was days — but once you jumped down from the train there was always the chance you'd be left behind, somewhere in Russia.

I grew quick and cunning, snatching whatever food I could find and taking it back to the wagon to share with Mama and Danuta. They seemed so sad and silent, huddling there together. It was as if they had lost hope. I brought them scraps of bread, a handful of wheat and some onions.

Once an old woman gave me a little piece of bacon fat. Even Mama smiled that day, but it was a shrunken skeleton's smile. She was getting thinner and thinner. Her eyes seemed to have sunk right back in her head.

As we travelled south it grew noticeably warmer, and we were eaten alive by lice. Typhoid and dysentery raged. Twenty or thirty people died every day and we had to leave them by the side of the railway track. After weeks in that wagon everyone was extremely weak and it became harder and harder to beg or steal. People in this part of the Soviet Union eked out a subsistence existence. They had nothing to share with these trainloads of desperate, starving Poles.

The boys in the wagon banded together, working as a scavenging party armed with knives and stones. I wanted to belong but they pushed me aside. Pawel, their leader, said that they did not want girls. They always brought back something to eat, even on the days when there was nothing in sight at the place where the train stopped. One night a boy gave me a handful of sticky dates. I stuffed them into my mouth, savouring the sweetness that brought back memories of life before the war.

We travelled further and further south. People were losing hope. It did not matter to anyone that so many people were dying. At each stop I closed my eyes to the piles of bodies, arms and legs, heads and feet, all jumbled together. It wasn't surprising that Mama got so sick when all around us people were dying. There was shit running all over the floor of the wagon. People sat and lay in the dirt. There was nowhere else to be. Mama lay on the floor moaning and vomiting. She was drenched with sweat from a raging fever. Danuta and I knelt beside her, trying to soothe her tossing head, trying to force water in between her lips. Danuta was crying and calling her name, 'Ludmilla, my little sister,' weeping as she tried to wash Mama's body with a rag dipped in water. There was nothing else we could do. Mama lay quite still. Her breaths were loud and rasping and she could not lift her head. When the train stopped Danuta wrapped her filthy shawl tightly around her shoulders.

'I am going to get help,' she said.

'How?' I asked her. I knew that we had no money and nothing left to sell, but Danuta would not talk to me. Maybe she had a ring or something she had kept hidden, I don't know.

My aunt got off the train and never came back. The train started up a few minutes after she'd climbed down on to the platform, and I was left alone with Mama in the wagon.

I didn't know what to do. I tried to clean Mama as best I could but she smelt really bad. Her breaths were coming in little gasps and moans. There was a ragged skirt in Auntie Danuta's bundle and I used it to wipe the vomit from Mama's face. She moaned when I touched her. I gave her our last sip of water but she could not swallow and it ran all over her face. I sat right beside her, smoothing the damp hair back from her forehead. When I was too tired to sit I lay beside her, trying to get under her arm as I used to when I was a small child. I must have gone to sleep under that arm because when I opened my eyes she was dead. Her body had gone very stiff and all the life had gone out of her.

The side of the wagon swung sideways, like a sliding door. It was dark outside. Nowhere. They lifted up my mother and put her on a stack of corpses right beside the railway line. Other bodies went on top of her. We left her there.

I don't remember what happened next. My mind was numb. I didn't know anyone, I wasn't hungry and I couldn't even remember my name. I had no boots, but someone gave me a pair which I saw being pulled off the body of a dead girl. They were too big for me, but I wore them anyway.

I do remember when the train stopped at Samarkand. It was the end of our long journey. People dragged themselves up from the floor and started to climb down from the wagon. I sat quite still, not knowing what to do, watching the woman who had been sitting on the floor next to me and Mama. She had two children with her and as she walked to the door of the wagon she turned to look at me.

'Chodz ze mna,' she said with a slight beckoning of her head.

I went with them. Pani Musinska, Aniela, Andrzej and me. We joined the shuffling crowd of Poles making their way to the Polish army headquarters. We stood in lines waiting to speak to the men in Polish army uniform standing behind a table. They seemed harassed and very busy. There was a never-ending queue of filthy, sick and starving refugees passing in front of them. The men asked me questions. I could not remember my name. I could not remember when

I was born. Pani Musinska gave my name as a member of her family as I stood shaking beside her. It was a relief to have someone to belong to.

The army authorities signed on the men and the boys who were fit enough to fight. Those who could prove that they had a father or brother in the army could register for army relief. For the rest of the people there was nothing. We were advised to move on out of that town.

I clung to the Musinska family, joining the stumbling column of Poles who were dragging themselves along the road. We walked on and on. Andrzej and I were always on the look-out for food. We had to steal. There was no other way of getting something to eat.

We were on the road to Bukhara. At night we slept in the local railway stations, lying in rows on the ground. In the morning officials would come and clear the place out and we walked on, looking for somewhere to go, for something to eat.

We came to the Amu Dar'ya River. There were huge flat barges travelling up and down the river and on the banks were a number of Soviet officials who loaded us aboard. We floated up the river, stopping at Uzbek villages along the way. Here and there officials ordered us to get off the barge, two or three Polish families at each stop. We stood on the bank of the river. It was hot and the bare earth was dry and dusty. I clung close to Pani Musinska and she let me hold her hand. The barge floated away and we were left there, at a *kolhoze* on the Amu Dar'ya River.

We left the riverbank and walked towards a village. All

around the earth was bare, even in the fields. There didn't seem to be anything to eat. In the village the women showed us an empty mud hut. It was called a *kibitka*. We went inside. There was nothing. At night we lay on the ground to sleep and in the morning Andrzej and I wandered through the village looking for food. Pani Musinska worked in the fields picking cotton. Every day she got a handful of grain in payment for her work. She boiled the grain with water and we each had two or three mouthfuls. Then it was all gone.

There was no bread in that place but one day Andrzej and I found an Uzbek woman cooking flat lumps of dough on an outdoor mud oven. We stood and watched, mesmerised by the smell and the sight of the balls of raw dough which stuck to the walls of the oven and fell to the ground when cooked. I wanted one of the dough balls more than anything else in the world. We stood and watched until the woman had finished cooking. She picked up the dough balls and went back to her hut. Andrzej and I scurried to her cooking place and sifted the dirt with our fingers, looking for any tiny crumb that might have dropped on the earth. I found three or four little bits that tasted of sand. My stomach cried out for more.

Once Andrzej stole a pumpkin. We saw it sitting in one of the fields, quite close to the fence, but during the day the fields were guarded. Andrzej waited until the middle of the night before creeping out to steal the pumpkin. When he brought it back to the hut we made a fire and cooked it straight away. I remember being surprised that it tasted so delicious because in Poland only animals ate pumpkin.

Slowly Andrzej and I became friends. At first we lived side by side, silent and watchful, careful to guard each mouthful of food in case the other stole it. We lay on the ground at night on either side of his mother and when she called us both 'moya kochana' I bit my lips to stop the tears falling because I knew she was not my mother.

It was the search for food that brought Andrzej and me closer together. Every day we went on scavenging expeditions, fishing in the river, stealing fruit and scouring the roads and ditches for something that we could eat. We stopped hiding food from each other and shared half of the smallest crust, saving the rest to take back to Andrzej's mother and sister. There was never enough to eat.

Some days I was too weak and tired to go out searching for food, so I sat in the hut with Aniela, who was always ill. But her illness reminded me of Mama's death and I had to go outside. I could not look at that little face lying there on the mud floor. It seemed as if everyone I knew got sick and died. I could no longer stand to watch their suffering.

One night I woke and heard Pani Musinska sobbing. Aniela was burning with fever. Andrzej tried to cool her with rags soaked in water from the river but it didn't seem to help. She died in her mother's arms. Pani Musinska cradled the body of her daughter until dawn, when Andrzej went outside to try to make a hole big enough to bury her.

Pani Musinska changed. She stopped going to work in the cotton fields, and walked around all day weeping silently. At night she sat awake staring into the darkness, crying and calling her daughter's name. Andrzej was worried. He tried to talk to his mother but she said nothing, and then one day she went down to the market to beg for food. When she came back she called to me and Andrzej.

'Come here and listen,' she said, putting her skinny arms around us. 'I have heard about an orphanage in Ashabad and I want you to go there.'

Her eyes were wide and shining. Andrzej and I looked at each other for a long time. We both loved Pani Musinska and did not want to leave her alone in this place. But she was excited, talking about what she had heard. 'They will feed you at the orphanage,' she said. 'And there will be bread. You must go Andrzej, and take Krystyna with you. Tell them she is your sister and that your mother is dead.'

We started to cry. Andrzej threw his arms around his mother and said that he would never leave her. I held the hand of the woman who had cared for me since Mama died, and wept bitterly. I wanted us to stay together and I wanted to go and get the bread that she was talking about.

We sat together all night, talking and crying. In the morning Pani Musinska untangled Andrzej's arms from around her waist and walked down to the river. We went and stood beside her. Soon the barge came. Pani Musinska took Andrzej into her arms one last time. She kissed him on his face and on his head.

'You must remember,' she said, 'that you are both Poles and that your parents are dead. You are on your way to the orphanage at Ashabad.'

We climbed into the barge and sailed downstream, sobbing and sobbing. I looked back as we rounded the corner and there was Pani Musinska's dear thin face, already fading into the distance.

On the barge Andrzej and I sat close together, crying. No one asked for our tickets or questioned our passage. When we reached Chardzhou we· got off the barge and walked through the streets to the railway station. There were people everywhere and no one noticed us. We stood alongside a family of Russians and boarded a train when they did. The mother looked at us but she did not smile. We sat on a seat near the door and looked out the window.

Soon the train started and a man came around asking for tickets. The Russian family had their tickets to show him but we had nothing. The man asked to see our papers. Andrzej told him that we had no parents and were going to the orphanage at Ashabad. I held Andrzej's hand and stared out the window.

'They are Poles,' the Russian woman said to the man collecting tickets, 'and they smell.'

The official stared at us, two dirty skinny children dressed in rags, and ordered us to get off at the next stop. Andrzej nodded. We had no money and no food. If we got off the train we would be lost, somewhere in the Soviet Union.

As soon as the official had left the carriage the Russian woman tapped Andrzej on the shoulder. He stiffened with fright, wondering what was going to happen, but the woman smiled and lifted up her skirts, motioning to us to climb underneath the seat she was sitting on. Her children watched as Andrzej and I crammed ourselves under the seat and the woman carefully spread her skirt in order to hide our legs. After a while the train stopped and the official came back to check on us. The woman pointed to our empty seat and thanked God that we had gone.

It was stuffy and crowded lying under the seat but Andrzej and I didn't mind. We were used to travelling in cramped conditions and after a while the woman handed a hunk of bread down to us. It was more food than we had seen for several days. We ate and lay curled up tightly together, listening to the endless clack-clack of the train on the rails.

After several hours the train stopped and the Russian woman peered down and started poking us, urging us to leave our hiding place. I was still tired. My head ached and my body felt hot and cold all over. I wanted to stay curled up on the floor, but Andrzej grabbed my hand and pulled me off the train. Once again we were on a strange platform. It was time to be quick and clever. People were being stopped on the station and asked for their papers. With an eye out for Russian soldiers, we threaded our way through the inevitable crowds, always trying to look as if we belonged to the people we were standing beside, but always moving on before they noticed us. My head was hurting so much I felt weak and dizzy. Andrzej held my hand and I followed, trying to ignore the nausea that rose in waves from the back of my throat.

'There's the gate!' Andrzej muttered at last. There didn't seem to be any soldiers guarding it but we both knew that in our dirty ragged clothes we would be very noticeable leaving the platform. Then Andrzej noticed a group of children walking towards the gate. Without a word we joined their line, keeping our heads down. No one pointed us out and we walked out into the street.

Ashabad seemed to be a big noisy town and we didn't know which way to go to find the orphanage. So for a long time we just sat in the park opposite the station looking at the paths and the green trees; somewhere near us there was water trickling softly. Suddenly Andrzej jumped up and ran away. I sat and watched him go. I thought that he must be leaving me there, but I didn't care. My head was aching. Then, dimly, as if through a haze, I saw Andrzej and a soldier walking towards me. I looked around, wondering where to run, where to hide, but it was too late. The soldier was standing there looking down at me. He had a Polish eagle on his cap.

'Come,' he said, lifting me up into his arms, 'I will take you to the orphanage where they will look after you.'

I remember lying still for a long time. People were calling my name but it did not mean anything to me. I saw the face of my mother. She was loving and kind, not thin and sad as she had been when she died. Sometimes I woke, aware of the fact that there were adults moving around. Someone was wiping my face with a cloth and brushing my hair. I was covered with something light and warm. I closed my eyes. I knew that I had died and that this was heaven.

I woke again in a strange place but this time I sat up and

looked around me. There were lots of children in the room, all lying in rows. I stood up and tried to walk but my legs buckled beneath me and I fell back onto the mattress. The girl who was lying next to me opened her eyes.

'Lie still, Zosia,' she said.

That was not my name. I wanted to tell her that it was wrong but the words would not come. My eyes closed and I slept some more. Then someone was shaking me, twisting my head from side to side. I opened my eyes and Andrzej was staring down at me. I seemed to remember his face from a long time ago.

'Quick Krysia,' he said, 'we are going and they are leaving the dying behind. You must get up and come with us.'

I didn't know what he was talking about. He pulled me upright but my legs wouldn't walk. I wanted to lie back down on the floor but Andrzej was impatient. He shook me so hard that I started crying.

'Listen to me,' Andrzej said, wiping the tears from my face. 'I promised Mama … I had to leave her but I am not leaving you.'

He brought me some clothes. Dirty rags. I don't know who they belonged to. I put them on and then I noticed that all around the room children were being dressed by their brothers, sisters or friends. There didn't seem to be any adults around. I wanted to ask what was happening but when I tried to speak my tongue stuck to the roof of my mouth.

As soon as I was dressed, Andrzej led me by the hand towards the door. We walked outside into the cool starry night where there were three or four trucks pulled up by the door. There seemed to be children everywhere, pulling each other up on to the open backs. Andrzej heaved me up and climbed on beside me. We sat very close and Andrzej held my hand. 'Where are we going?' I asked him. I was tired and my legs were shaking. It was a long time since I had done any walking. Andrzej put his arms around me.

'Listen, little sister,' he said, 'we are leaving Russia.'

I didn't believe him. I lifted my head to stare into his face. His eyes were shining.

I didn't realise it at the time, but without Andrzej's help I would have been left there in the Soviet Union. In January 1943 the amnesty that had let us go free from the labour camps was cancelled. All the Poles who were living in the territory annexed by the Soviet Union were to become Soviet citizens. Anyone who refused to renounce their Polish citizenship was arrested and sent to a prison or labour camp. The Poles who were running the orphanage where I lay sick were all arrested, but by some miracle the children were allowed to go free. We climbed on to those trucks and began another journey. No one knew where we were going. We were a truckload of children without a future.

We were driven to Krasnovodsk, a port on the Caspian Sea. It was a long bumpy journey and most of the time I lay on the floor, too sick to care where we were going. After two or three days the motor stopped grinding over the rough roads and we climbed down from the back of the truck. Almost immediately we were surrounded by Polish voices.

There were people everywhere, hundreds and thousands of Polish people trying to get a place on a boat, desperate to cross the Caspian Sea and leave the Soviet Union behind forever.

The children from our truck clung together, a forlorn little group among so many desperate people. Then, from somewhere among this mass of wailing and shouting, a group of Polish soldiers appeared. They ordered us to stand in lines and led us through the crowd towards the beach. We walked two by two, one behind the other, and although people moved to let us through I was frightened by the press of the crowd around us. You could feel desperation in the air. No one wanted to be left behind, but in order to leave you had to have papers showing that you were a member of an army family or that you belonged to an orphanage. People jostled against us. They grabbed our arms and shouted into our faces, pleading with us to help them. A woman leaned forward and put a baby in my arms. It had a little piece of paper tied around its neck. I looked around for the mother of the baby but in that sea of faces there was no one I could recognise. The baby was crying.

We climbed up a ramp and on to a boat with a large open deck. A man asked our names and crossed them off a list. He took no notice of the baby. I wished that I did not have to carry it along. I was so tired and the baby was heavy. Andrzej was a long way in front of me, walking with the other boys. I called to him but in the roar of the crowd he did not hear.

The boat deck was already crowded. The soldiers urged

us towards the middle but there were so many of us packed together that we couldn't move. I held the baby, leaning its weight up against the people who were standing in front of me. The terrible sound of crying wafted towards us from the shore. People were pleading to be allowed to board. I couldn't see above the people who were wedged in around me but slowly, slowly I could feel the boat pulling away from the shore. I stood on the deck looking up at the sky. The light had faded to a deep blue but its beauty meant nothing to me. The press of people meant that you could not sit down. My arms ached from holding on to the baby.

The boat wallowed in the water, so laden with passengers that the waves washed over the deck. The wind blew all around us and as we got further out to sea the waves rose higher and the boat tossed about. People were being washed off the sides. For a minute or two you could see them sliding down the huge waves and then they were gone. Fear gripped us by the throat. People fell to the deck and were trampled by those around them. You could not see where to put your feet and the tossing of the boat made your footing unsteady. The screaming and shouting was shrill in the wind. The baby was crying. Its small body was wet and I could not read the name that was written on the paper around its neck.

After a while the swell died down and people settled themselves as best they could. Andrzej fought his way through the crowd to stand beside me. He looked at the baby and shook his head but he took a turn to hold it in his arms. Somewhere in the middle of the boat people began singing Polish hymns. The familiar words spread through the crammed boat, calming the panic. Soon everyone was singing and crying and praying. We had left the Soviet Union behind us. I stood on the deck and held the baby, wondering what would happen to us now.

We arrived in Pahlevi. The sun was hot, beating down on our heads, but there was a warm gentle breeze that was soft against your face. We walked off the boat and were taken to a large Red Cross tent. Andrzej lined up with the other boys. I stood in the girls' line. A woman took the baby from my arms. She asked me its name but I just shook my head. The paper with the child's name on it had blown away.

The line moved forwards and we were led into the tent. It was full of thin girls standing in rows. No one spoke. A woman dressed in white told us to take off our clothes and leave them in a pile beside the door. The girl standing beside me did not want to take off her dress. She whispered that it had belonged to her mother. The woman in white sighed. Then she tugged the ragged dress up over the girl's shoulders and left her standing there, crying and naked. Men with big gloves came to the door of the tent. They scooped up the piles of dirty clothes and took them away. The woman in white said that our clothes were full of disease and had to be burned.

We were all given a piece of soap. I bit mine to see if it was good to eat but the taste was awful and it burned my mouth. We stood in lines and then walked to the showers. There was warm water trickling out of a nozzle and it made tracks through the dirt on my body. I washed myself carefully. I couldn't remember ever having washed in warm water before.

After the shower we were given garments that looked like white tents. We stood in lines while the woman in white went around with big scissors cutting off our braids. Then a man shaved off all the rest of our hair. The woman in white said that it was to make sure that all the lice died. I reached up and ran my hands over my head. It felt ugly. Andrzej was standing in the boys' line. He looked so different without any hair. I wanted to run over and stand beside him, but his line moved away and Andrzej disappeared among the other boys with shaven heads. I felt lonely without him.

We sat in open tents on the sand. Women in white dresses gave us bread to eat and water to drink. We waited for whatever would happen next. At nightfall each of us was given a red blanket. I sat on mine so that no one would take it from me. It was the first thing I had owned for a long time.

Someone said my name. It echoed far off in a distant consciousness. Somewhere far away in the back of my mind I remembered being that girl, but now things were different. I belonged to this group of children with shaven heads, sitting on the sand.

Life happened as it did. I watched it pass, but I didn't really feel as if I was there. I couldn't talk or play. I no longer wondered what would happen next. Every day was the same, sitting there on the sand in the warm breeze. People seemed kind. There was no beating and shouting. Life seemed to have a gentleness that I had never known before. All day I listened to the egg sellers shouting, 'Hard-boiled eggs for sale,' and I thought it was strange that the hens in this place laid eggs that were already boiled.

We moved on again, climbing up into the back of army trucks en route to Isfahan. It did not matter to me where we were going. I just went with the rest of the children, doing whatever they were doing. American soldiers helped us to climb aboard. They were laughing and talking, throwing the smallest children up into the air. One of them gave me a bar of chocolate. I did not know what to do with it, even though the soldier tore off the wrapper and tried to put the chocolate in my mouth. I did not know that it was food. I ate only bread. I hoped that we would be going somewhere there would be bread tomorrow.

# The Second Journey

I follow my mother into these God-forsaken places and see now the face of a survivor. I see the shuttered sadness that lies beside her every night, and the dark memories of life without any future.

I ask her about how she came to New Zealand, after surviving the chaos of those long train journeys. My mother sighs and looks out the window. She says that it was by chance that she came to live in this country. There were hundreds of children without names or parents and she was among them. I follow her back into that story.

# Chapter 6

I came back to myself in an orphanage on the edge of a new world. Every day long lists of children's names were put up on the notice-board and at the top of the list were the names of faraway destinations, places across the sea in other parts of the world. All around me children were getting ready to go to countries like Canada, Africa, America and Israel.

At night we lay in bed and talked about which country we would like to go to. Poland was our first choice but the war was still on and we could not go home. We had to go somewhere else until the fighting was over.

Life in Teheran had an order and an easiness to it. Slowly the children around me changed from lice-bitten skeletons into thin serious people. I guess that I looked the same, but my body was dead to me now. All I wanted was to get enough to eat every day, to sit under the trees and to close off the places in my mind where there was sadness and hunger, screaming and crying. Every day we had Mass outside under the trees. We stood in lines and sang hymns in Polish that reached back into the life that I had lived a long time ago. At nights I longed for my mother's arms to be around me.

In the afternoons we had classes in an empty aircraft hangar. It was cool and our voices echoed loudly as we chanted our lessons aloud in Polish. There were no books. Our teachers taught us what they could remember. Sometimes when they talked about their lives in Poland it all whirled around in my head in a mix of facts and folk tales. I wasn't sure what I'd been told and what I could remember, but it didn't seem to matter. The main thing was to get on with the business of living and being Polish.

One morning my name was written up on the noticeboard. I was on the list of children to go to New Zealand. I ran to Siostra Ludwika, the nurse, and asked if she knew where New Zealand was.

'It is a little country at the end of the world,' she said, patting my shoulder. 'You will be happy there.'

But her words didn't really reassure me and rumours spread. Someone told me that there were cannibals in New Zealand. Great big people with enormous mouths and blood dripping from their jaws. At night I couldn't sleep. I saw that I would have to be very careful in New Zealand so that the eating people didn't take a bite out of me.

At classes in the aircraft hangar I asked the teacher

about New Zealand. She smiled and said that it was a country flowing with milk and honey. I imagined that everyone would have a little cup to dip into the golden flowing streams. I knew that if I could keep away from the eating people I would not be hungry there.

Now I was separated from the main group and became one of the children who was going to New Zealand. As we gathered together for special lessons I looked around at the other children who were going to the end of the world with me. They had shaven heads and serious faces, all turned towards Kierownieczka Nowacka.

'You are being given shelter in New Zealand until the end of the war,' she said, 'but I want you always to remember that you are Polish.'

'But what will happen after the war?' one of the boys asked.

'The little soldiers will return to the homeland,' she said. 'We will all return to Poland.'

After weeks of anticipation we left Teheran very early one morning, climbing into army trucks after our names were crossed off a list. There were rows of benches in the back of the truck, and we sat in the middle rows while the teachers who were going with us had the seats against the wall. I clutched the board seat and stared at the wall, trying not to see the woman who sat opposite me with her arm encircling her daughter. There was no one to put their arm around me on the way to New Zealand. I closed my eyes and tried to cover the sadness.

We drove to Basra where we boarded a ship. Two by two up the gangplank and down the stairs into the hold. The air was hot and dank. We lay on mattresses on the floor but it was so hot it was hard to breathe. Sweat ran down my face and neck. I was desperate for a drink of water.

In the middle of the night one of the teachers helped us to carry the mattresses up on to the deck. Hundreds of bright stars lit up the sky and the sea air was fresh and salty. We lay there under the stars, listening to the chug of the ship's engine as it took us further and further away from the war in our occupied homeland.

In the morning I woke suddenly to the whoosh of cold water across my face. The British sailors were washing the deck shouting, 'Wakey, wakey, rise and shine.' I scrambled to my feet and rushed to haul my mattress out of the way. We ate dried fish and bread for breakfast. The fish was so salty that it made my throat burn, and the drinking water tasted oily. But it didn't matter: we were on our way to New Zealand where I would be able to dip my cup in the stream of milk and honey.

Our ship sailed into port at Bombay, where we climbed down one gangplank and up another, on to a huge, gleaming American troopship called the *General Randall*. 'Welcome aboard, welcome aboard,' the American soldiers said as we boarded the ship. They chucked us under the chin and handed out huge slabs of no-melt chocolate. You could keep it in your pocket for days. There were both New Zealand and American soldiers aboard the *General Randall*. The Americans staffed the huge warship while the New

Zealanders took it easy below the decks. They were battle fatigued and glad to be returning home after months of fighting the European war.

Each of us had a bunk of our own, with a pillow and soft blankets. The ship was so huge that you could hardly hear the motors but it was easy to turn down the wrong corridor and get lost. Sometimes on the way to bed we'd walk into a huge bunkroom full of men. They whistled and sat us on their laps, filled our pockets with chewing gum and tickled us under the chin. I sat beside a man who kept screwing up his face and laughing in a big loud voice.

'Come on, kiddie, smile,' he said.

I stared while he twisted his cheeks, poked out his tongue and rolled his eyes around in his head. He waved his arms and crowed out loud like a rooster in the farmyard. I stared until he flopped down onto the bunk.

'Can't understand it,' he said, looking worried. 'Why don't you kids smile?'

I often saw that soldier on the deck, flapping his arms and making faces. There were always children standing watching, waiting until he had finished, when he would hand out chocolate or chewing gum. He asked us to call him 'Uncle New Zealand'.

Sometimes the soldiers took a turn in the ship's galley and piled our plates high with huge mounds of smooth white potato with a chunk of butter on top.

'Gotta get some meat on your bones,' they said. 'You kids will come right with a decent Kiwi roast.'

It certainly was easier to feel happy with food in your

stomach, and gradually the terrible things that had happened started to seem further away. I still longed for my mother and carefully watched the children whose mothers had come with us, envying their kisses and caresses. I wished that there was someone to comfort me, but in that crowd of children I learnt to look after myself.

Every three or four days the sirens shrilled and we had drill. The American soldiers, carrying hoses and wearing fire-fighting equipment, ran backwards and forwards all over the ship. We had to stand in lines in the bunkroom, and sometimes we were called up on to the deck to practise climbing into the lifeboats which were winched out from the side of the ship and lowered into the sea. The waves splashed around us and we could look up and see the ship towering above us.

Two or three times during the voyage the sirens made a different noise, an urgent screeching that set our teeth on edge. 'Sub attack!' the soldiers shouted. We rushed downstairs and lay on our beds, terrified that the ship would be blown apart. Our teachers led us in prayers and songs until the all-clear sounded. It was such a relief to go on living. I was scared of ending up floating in the deep blue sea.

I was one of hundreds of Polish children on that ship. We ate and played together, getting to know each other's faces. Every day the priest said Mass and we stood on the deck holding hands and singing the sad hymns of our homeland. We wept as we sang because our songs were of our beloved country and now we were sailing to the end of the world. Our teachers called us 'na wygnancy', the people dispossessed of their homeland, and we held tightly to each other because we knew we carried our Polishness with us. Slowly the other children became familiar companions. We learnt each other's names and helped the younger children to get dressed in the morning. Being together dimmed the aching loss of our mothers and sisters, our fathers and brothers and our homes. These people were all the family that was left to us now.

After weeks at sea the *General Randall* sailed into the port of Wellington, New Zealand. The New Zealand soldiers were up on deck all night, singing and shouting as they watched the land come closer and closer. They practised rugby on the deck, throwing around a funny oval ball and pushing each other over so that they could grab it. As we sailed into the harbour they grew even louder with excitement. They clapped and cheered and did their haka. All around, the steep green hills were closing in and the sun was fiercely bright above us. We could see that the hills were covered with brightly coloured houses with brightly coloured roofs. Looking up, I chose a little red roof for myself. Perhaps in this country everyone had a house of their own. Everything was strange, and quite different from anywhere we'd been before. We stood on the deck in the biting wind, staring out at the hills and the harbour. The soldiers crowded against the rails of the ship. Down below us on the wharf hundreds of people were waving and cheering. The men on the deck were waving back, pointing out people they knew. We stood together, watching. We knew that the bands and the cheering were not for us. I thought of my father who rode away to war so long ago, and I wondered where he was now.

The New Zealand soldiers threw their kit bags over their shoulders and marched off down the gangplank. Then an old man climbed on board, followed by three or four men and women who looked at us and smiled.

'Children, this is Prime Minister Peter Fraser,' a man said.

'Welcome, children,' Peter Fraser said.

He walked around the deck patting children on the head while people took photographs. I thought that he looked like a kind man, even though I could not understand what he was saying. He was wearing a hat with the brim turned up at the edge and he watched as we lined up and walked off the ship, waving goodbye to the American soldiers who loaded our pockets with chocolate and chewing gum. One of them tweaked my cheek.

'See ya, kid,' he said.

For a long time I practised those words over and over until I could say them with a convincing American twang. 'See ya … see ya … see ya.'

People crowded around as we walked, one behind the other, down the gangplank and into a huge draughty building where we lined up for medical inspection. Men in white coats looked through our hair. We took off our clothes and they thumped our chests. They stared into our eyes and down our throats. I wished they would leave us alone. We put on our clothes and walked into another room. All around us people were staring and talking in a language that we could not understand. Women who looked like big soft mattresses gave each of us a cardboard box tied with string. I opened mine straight away. Inside there were some sandwiches and a piece of pink cake. I crammed the food into my mouth, but there wasn't time to eat. Already the line was moving and we were walking outside again. I put the pink cake in my pocket with the gum and chocolate.

We walked across the wharf to a railway platform. Everywhere there were huge crowds of people, pointing and waving. Boys with green caps and scarves handed us packets of food. We climbed into a proper railway carriage. There were seats and windows so that you could look outside. Hundreds of faces pressed up against the window, talking and pointing. They pushed things through the windows at the top of the carriage — sweets, soft squashy cakes and flat pieces of money. Our teachers said they were called pennies and I put one in my pocket.

The train hooted its whistle and jerked to a start. We sat on the seats with food piled around us, staring out as the train moved on. The countryside was unlike anything we had seen before. Rounded green hills, criss-crossed with little mud tracks, crouched low alongside the railway tracks. Everywhere there were lots of fat white woolly animals with pointy faces. Our teachers called them sheep. Then the train clattered around the side of a hill and suddenly we saw the sea. A huge expanse of brilliant blue water stretched before us with an island sitting in the middle. We forgot about the food and stared at the sea and the rugged rocks that tumbled along the shoreline. It was a wild and beautiful place with the smell of salt spray strong in the air, but the emptiness was still inside me. The seascape, the swirling seagulls, the cakes and lunch boxes couldn't reach it.

Two hours later we reached Palmerston North station. Again there were crowds of people waving and cheering. Again we held hands and followed the New Zealand soldiers who helped us up into the back of open-air trucks where we sat side by side looking down on the people crowding below us. As soon as the truck was full, three or four women climbed up and started handing us things.

'Ice cream,' they said, smiling.

I held my ice cream tight, staring at the tiny pink, green and blue sweets sprinkled on the top.

'Hundreds and thousands,' one of the women said, pointing at the melting colours.

I realised that you were supposed to eat them, but my stomach felt tight and sort of squishy. The girl sitting beside me took a bite from hers and the cone snapped. Splat! There was her ice cream lying on the floor. A woman bent to clean it up. She looked cross as she scraped the sticky stuff on to a brown piece of paper.

'Oh well,' she said, 'they don't know any better.'

I started to eat mine in a hurry because I didn't want to make that lady mad. The ice cream was all soft and there were trails of it running down my hands. In three bites I managed to swallow it, rubbing my sticky hand on the bottom of my skirt.

'Did you see that?' the lady said to one of the soldiers. She came over and put her face very close to mine. 'You don't bite ice cream, you lick it … see …' and she started making huge swoops with her big pink tongue. I sat, staring, because I had never seen anyone as fat as she was. There were rolls of spare flesh under her chin, and her arms wobbled as she talked. For as long as I could remember I had seen thin people with bones sticking out of their bodies. I wondered what had happened to this lady's bones.

The army trucks started up and we drove out of town and up the hills and valleys of the Pahiatua Track. The countryside was green and peaceful. Sheep grazed in the fields, but there were no people. Occasionally we drove past a house or into a tiny town where a handful of women and children stood waving and cheering, and then at last we drove into Pahiatua, the place we knew was going to be our home in New Zealand. Here the streets were crowded shoulder to shoulder with people who waved and shouted as we drove past. At the top of the main street a band was playing and lines of men in uniform stood to attention. Then we drove out of the town and along a country road. The trucks turned left, bumping off the road, and we went through the gates of a huge compound with a sign that said 'Pahiatua Camp'.

It seemed like somewhere we had been before, another internment camp with wooden barracks in an empty field surrounded by barbed wire. We stared at the long rows of buildings and the soldiers standing in lines, and wondered if life would be better in this place. The sky was wide above us and all around were grassy fields stretching as far as the glowing mountains on the horizon.

Women in white dresses organised us into lines and led us into the wooden buildings. There were long rows of beds inside, one bed for each of us with a mat on the floor and a dressing table on the right. A woman in white pulled open the drawers of the dressing table. There was newspaper on the bottom neatly folded into the corners.

'Now unpack your things,' she said, making unfolding motions with her hands.

I stood and watched, feeling vaguely uncomfortable. Some of the children had brought a small bundle with them, but I had nothing. When the woman in white was busy elsewhere I carefully shut the wooden drawers. Maybe one day I would find something to put inside them.

On the top of each dressing table there was a jug of milk and some bread. After all the drawers were shut the woman in white pointed to the bread. We ate. White bread was like cake to us and this had a crust on top and a soft spongy middle. In Siberia, bread had always been dark dry hunks. You gnawed it and saved the crumbs. I ate the tender middle of my beautiful New Zealand bread and hid the crusts under the clean white pillow on my bead. It was good to know that there would be something to eat tomorrow.

Life at Pahiatua Camp settled down to a regular pattern. From the first day, food was an important part of it. We ate all our meals in the dining room, which was a separate wooden building in the long row of barracks. There was bread, butter and milk for breakfast and meat for dinner — hunks of meat that tasted strong and chewy. After the meat we had wobbly coloured puddings that were sweet and empty. The New Zealand soldiers called it jelly.

Sometimes we would hang around the kitchen until the soldiers put the rubbish out and we'd hunt through the bins to see what we could get. There might be bones to gnaw or pieces of stale bread, but the best find of all was a butter paper. We would run and hide in the long grass, taking turns to lick the folds, gloating over the sweet, salty taste. We also had bread parties in our dormitories at night, feasting on bread we'd saved and kept in our bedside drawers until we had a big pile.

The days were predictable but I liked the routine. They blocked out the numbness that always lurked in the back of my mind. We lived in the barracks with other girls or boys about our own age. We had to rise at six o'clock every morning and wash ourselves in the ablutions block where there were rows of baths made of grey flaky tin that burnt your backside when you sat down. We had great pieces of yellow soap and I loved to lather my arms and legs and watch the dirt being smoothed away. Every time I had a bath I felt as if I was being made new.

Saturday was the worst day of the week because that was when we had lice inspection. Once we had lice crawling all over our bodies, but here it was different. There was a sense of shame in having lice on your neck or in your hair. The nurses looked through every inch of our heads and if they found a louse you had to comb your hair with kerosene for a whole week. The smell was terrible and everyone knew who had lice because of the stink.

Most days we played outside in the paddocks, running through the grass and climbing all over the Pahiatua grand-stand which had rows of wooden seats that stretched high in the sky. Soon our clothes were in tatters, and our Polish teachers took the problem very seriously. They tried to keep us clean and tidy but we looked like some sort of ragged band. One morning there were no classes. Instead we had to line up in the assembly area where there were six or seven women soldiers standing behind a huge pile of clothes. We filed past them slowly and as we came to the top of the line one of the women picked out an item of clothing and held it in the air. When it was my turn, the woman gave me a quick sideways glance, handed over the garment and then pulled out something else woolly to go with it.

Back in the dormitories we tried on our new clothes. Nothing fitted. I had a huge black dress with splits under the armpits. It dragged on the ground when I walked. The woolly thing was a cardigan. The sleeves ended at my elbows and there weren't any buttons, but it was a beautiful pale blue and I loved it. Up and down the dormitory we paraded our new clothes. We looked like some sort of clown circus in our mismatched, odd-sized cast-offs, but they were better than the rags we had just stepped out of and now we had something to wear for the prime minister's visit.

For weeks we had been practising Polish songs and dances. Our teachers had spent long evenings in the kitchen preparing cakes and other delicacies. On the day of his visit we were all up early, sweeping the parade ground and decorating the barracks with garlands that we had made

140

from coloured paper. We felt that Peter Fraser was our friend, and as he drove into the camp we stood in the road cheering and waving.

The prime minister stood to address us on the garlanded outdoor stage but we could not understand his words. He smiled as he listened to our singing and watched our dancing. He ate Polish cakes and said '*Dobri*' which made us laugh. It was like having a good father to visit.

After he left, the teachers told us that Peter Fraser was going to send us new clothes. We were surprised by this, because the clothes we were wearing were still new, to us. All the same, three weeks later we were each given a brown paper parcel. Inside there were two sets of cotton khaki uniforms. The boys had shorts and shirts, while the girls were given two wraparound dresses with lots of pockets. The fabric was stiff and new and the dresses had strings which you could pull tight around your body if you were small or let out if you were bigger. Then we lined up for new shoes. The soldiers looked at our feet and handed over a pair of shoes with leather like sizzled bacon. They didn't fit. Some girls managed to swap around for a pair the right size, but no one wanted to swap with me because the shoes I had been given were huge. I had to wear them on Sundays and whenever we had parade, so I stuck my feet right up the front and ignored the clomping noise they made as I walked along.

We became fastidious about looking after our new khaki uniforms. Everyone had the same method and each night we would wash one dress in the bath and put it under

141

the mattress so that in the morning it would be pressed flat. We kept our old clothes in the chests of drawers and wore them on Sundays after Mass.

Sunday was the busiest day of the week. From ten o'clock in the morning people from outside the camp would drive their cars in through the gates, staring and pointing. At twelve o'clock they would get a picnic basket from the back of the car and eat lunch. At three o'clock they would have sandwiches and cakes with tea from a thermos, staring about while they were eating and drinking. I guess they wanted to see what we looked like but I hated being stared at. I'd try and hide in the toilets for hours. Sometimes I'd run past their cars shouting rudely in Polish. That gave them something to stare at.

If it weren't for Sundays, life at Pahiatua Camp would have been like being in a little Poland. Our classes were in Polish and although we had one English lesson a week we knew very little about our new country. We stared at the New Zealanders and they stared back at us, but we had very little to do with each other until our teachers announced that we were going on farm holidays, to stay with kind New Zealand friends.

Two weeks later we were dispatched on the Pahiatua train, each of us with a big ticket pinned to the front of our khaki uniform. Mine said 'MACE', which was the name of the family with whom I was going to stay. I sat on the train and practised my New Zealand words. 'Thank you very much.' 'Good morning.' 'Goodbye.'

At Masterton there was a small wooden building and a

tiny platform crowded with people who rushed towards us as we climbed down from the train. Men and women kept pushing each other aside as they grabbed the front of our uniforms to read the name that was written there. A man put his hand on my shoulder. There was a girl with him about the same size as me.

'Come on,' said the man, 'let's get outta here.' He gave me a little push so I picked up my things and followed them. The man walked very quickly, with huge steps. The girl was skipping along beside him. Every now and then she turned to look at me and smiled. I felt reassured by her smile even though I was nervous and frightened.

The man and the girl climbed into the front of a big black car and the girl leaned over the seat and pointed to the back door. I climbed inside and heaved my suitcase after me. The man started up the engine and lit a cigarette. I sat right beside the window, looking out as we drove through the town and out into the countryside. There were fields and fences on both sides of the road and every now and then we ran over a squashed animal.

'Bloody possums,' the man said. I wondered what sort of dead animal it was, and whether or not you could eat it.

It was late afternoon when we reached the house, which sat in the middle of a paddock with untidy clumps of arum lilies growing along the sides.

'Gotta see to the cows,' the man said, pulling up in front of the house. He disappeared around the back.

The girl turned around and smiled. Then she opened the car door, and, taking my hand, led me into the house.

There was no one home and the rooms smelt stale and empty. There were blowflies buzzing against the windows in the kitchen. I stood in the middle of the floor and waited, wondering what had happened to the rest of the people who lived in the house. The girl clambered up on to the wooden bench and opened a cupboard near the roof. She took out a rusty tin and shook it.

'Biscuits,' she said, and jumped down. Inside the tin there were some brown biscuits stuck together with jam. 'Belgians,' the girl said, and she held the tin out towards me. I took a biscuit and began to eat. It was soft, tasting vaguely of cinnamon.

'Thank you,' I said.

'You're all right,' the girl said, smiling at me. 'I reckon we'll get on okay together.'

I smiled back with my mouth full. The house seemed strange but there was something reassuring about the girl's friendliness. She grabbed my hand and led me down the passageway to a small room with faded red roses on the wall. There were piles of dead flies on the windowsills and the bed was sagging in the middle.

'You'll sleep here,' she said, 'but you'll have to share with Molly.'

I wasn't sure what the girl meant but she smiled and bounced on the bed with her bottom neatly tucked into the sag of the springs. I climbed into the sag and sat beside her. Soon we were both bouncing and giggling, daring each other to bounce higher. Dust rose from the old kapok mattress and the bedsprings creaked furiously. We bounced until we were breathless from giggling and then we climbed off the bed and went back into the kitchen for another belgian.

After we'd eaten, the girl climbed on a stool and started rummaging about in the cupboards. I liked the fact that she was living here alone so boldly, but I wondered where her mother was. The whole house seemed quiet and empty. There was dust in all the corners and the floors were black with dirt. I looked around the kitchen trying to find some small trace of the girl's mother but there was nothing. The girl darted around the kitchen opening cupboards and banging drawers.

'I'm gonna get the stew on,' she said. 'Dad likes a bit of stew for his tea.'

She chopped an onion and a couple of parsnips into tiny pieces, put them into a saucepan with a cup of water, and turned the stove on. Then she grabbed my hand and led me outside across the grass where she showed me the woodshed and a tumbledown building where her father was wearing big black gumboots and plugging pumps onto the hanging-down udders of huge cows. He looked up and nodded his head as we stood watching.

'Machine-milking, eh?' he said, winking.

I could hear the milk going *shoog … shoog … shoog* down the hoses. The girl led me over to a stainless steel vat where the milk was swirling around the sides. I watched, fascinated, while the cows kept munching and letting go huge green streams of cow ploop. The shed had a warm, animally sort of smell and seemed a happier place to be than the sad wooden house with the blowflies piled up in the corners.

I felt someone tugging my arm. 'Let's go,' the girl said. 'Better get the meat on.'

She ran through the long grass towards the house and I followed her as closely as I could, jumping over the dried cow turds and trying not to lose sight of my footing. Then the girl disappeared around the side of the house and for a moment I was alone in the field under the huge sky. The smell of grass in the wind reminded me of Poland, but somehow everything seemed strange. The sun was in the wrong place in the sky and there were no other houses around. I ran as fast as I could, trying to find the girl. She was standing in front of a meat safe hanging in a tree, and as I ran towards her she held out a big chunk of red meat.

'It's our own,' she said, holding the meat out for me to admire.

I couldn't look at it. The redness made me feel sick.

'What's the matter?' the girl asked, nudging me with her shoulder.

'Thank you very much,' I said and turned away.

The girl laughed and shut the meat safe.

'Let's go inside,' she said. 'We've gotta get the meat on.'

She led the way through the back door and into the kitchen where she put the meat on a wooden board and started chopping it into small pieces. I stood watching until she handed me a knife and six large dirty potatoes.

'You do the spuds,' she said and carried on chopping.

I wasn't sure what she wanted me to do. At Pahiatua Camp all our meals were prepared for us, and it was a long time since I had been in my mother's kitchen. But I took the knife and copied what the girl was doing, cutting the potatoes into small, even-sized pieces.

'Cor,' she said when she saw me chopping. 'What d'you think you're doing?'

I put the knife down and looked at the floor. 'Goodbye,' I said.

The girl grabbed my arm with her meaty hands. 'Jeez,' she said, 'I'm sorry. I didn't know that you can't peel spuds.' She peered into my face with such a look of concern that I smiled at her and everything was all right again. 'Tell you what,' she said, 'why don't you have a look at Mum's photograph album while I get dinner on?'

She steered me over to a couch which was covered with a faded plaid blanket, and pushed a leather-bound book into my hands. I couldn't read the words because they were written in English but I turned the pages and stared at pictures of men and women, children and babies, smiling at the camera. I guessed that somewhere in this book there would be a photograph of the girl's mother but I peered into all the faces and none of them seemed to resemble the girl. A warm smell of meat and potatoes filled the kitchen. I sat there turning the pages and watching the girl as she set the table, scrubbed down the chopping board and peeled some carrots. As evening started to darken the room she switched on the electric light and the man came inside, bringing with him the smell of milk and animals.

'Tea's ready,' the girl said, taking the photograph album from my knees. 'Wash your hands in there,' and she pointed towards the concrete tub just inside the back door.

The man sat down and started eating. I sat down at the table and the girl put a plate of meat, potatoes and carrots in front of me.

'Thank you,' I said.

She smiled, but no one spoke. The three of us sat together and ate.

As soon as the man had finished he lit a cigarette and inhaled deeply. 'All right, you two,' he said, 'better get going.'

The girl gobbled her last forkful and gathered up my empty plate. 'Visiting time,' she said.

I jumped up from the table, wondering what was going to happen next. The man walked towards the back door and grabbed a hat on the way out.

'Come on,' said the girl. 'Let's go.'

It was dark outside, but the air still smelt warm and grassy. The man started up the car and this time the girl climbed into the back seat beside me. She seemed nervous and kept biting her lip as the man guided the car back down the track that led to the farm.

'I wish I'd brought some flowers,' the girl said, leaning over the front seat close to her father.

'Haven't got any,' the man said.

'Those arums would do,' the girl told him.

He laughed loudly, throwing back his head. 'There's plenty of time for arums,' he said. 'Just wait a few months till she's dead.'

We drove back the way we had come that afternoon, all the way into Masterton and then around the back of the township to a large group of buildings. The man parked the car and we walked inside. The smell was antiseptic and seemed familiar. We walked down a long dark corridor, the girl and her father in front while I trailed along behind them. Then they turned left into a small green room where there was a woman lying on a bed.

'Hello, Mum,' the girl said, bending down to kiss the stick-like figure on the forehead.

'I've brought the girl,' her husband said. 'Seems to get on okay with Joan.'

He took my elbow and pushed me forwards towards the bed. I stared down at the face that was lying there on the pillows. She looked so small and her thin hands plucked continuously at the blankets of the bed.

'Good morning,' I said and curtsied as we had been taught to do at Pahiatua Camp.

The woman raised her head from the pillow and burst out laughing, a thin cackle of laughter that turned into a fit of coughing. Her daughter held her up while she coughed and then lowered her gently back on to the pillows.

'Well, blow me down,' the sick woman said once she had got her breath back. 'Tell me, kiddie ... do they have cows in Poland?'

I didn't know what she was saying so I just shook my head. All three of them were staring at me so hard that I felt a hot blush of embarrassment rising up my neck and across my face. I knew that for some reason they thought I was amusing and I wanted to get away from their staring faces. In three steps backwards I was out the door and standing in the dark, antiseptic-smelling corridor. Inside I could hear them talking, the girl quick and fast, the man slow and drawling, and the sick lady low in the middle. Nurses in white dresses walked up and down the corridor, glancing quickly at me as they passed. I felt very lonely standing there while the girl was inside the room with her mother and father, but I bit my lips and tried not to cry.

Going back to Pahiatua Camp was like returning home. We sat around on our beds in the barracks, talking together in the language that was our own. Our experiences outside had brought us closer together and the camp was a place where we belonged. In the New Zealand world we were lost and lonely. Anything could happen.

I concentrated on my lessons, trying to do well in class. The teachers praised my Polish. I wanted to excel so that I would be safe from the New Zealand world where I felt so out of place. Soon I was top of my class and whenever an important person came to visit the camp I was chosen to make a speech on behalf of all the Polish children. I smiled and curtsied and handed over bunches of flowers. Men patted my head and women kissed my cheek. It was easy to smile at them. At Pahiatua I knew that I was one of the Polish children and I wanted to stay there forever.

One afternoon my teacher asked me to come to her house after class. This was a great honour. I washed my face, combed my hair and changed into the clean damp khaki uniform that was lying under the mattress on my bed. The teachers at Pahiatua Camp lived in small square buildings that were separate from the rest of us. They had a bedroom, a sitting room and a small kitchen all to themselves and their families. My teacher, Madame Swietlicka, came to greet me as I knocked at the door.

'*Dzien dobri*, Krystyna,' she said. 'Please come inside.'

There were three other girls already there. I smiled and said, '*Dzien dobri*.' They were older than me and belonged to the next dormitory. I felt nervous and excited, wondering why I had been called to join them. Madame Swietlicka poured us tea with lemon and offered around a plate of cakes. I took one but was too excited to eat. The chocolate icing started to melt as I held the cake in my hand and the hot lemon tea scalded my throat. Madame Swietlicka chatted about the camp and her husband in Poland whom she had located through the International Red Cross. She hoped that he would be able to join her in New Zealand. For a moment I had a whisper of hope that someone from my family had also been found and we would be reunited.

'Now, girls,' Madame Swietlicka said briskly once everyone had finished their tea. 'I have something very important to tell you.' We all sat with our hands folded, staring at her expectantly. She smiled at us and started to speak rapidly in Polish. 'The New Zealand authorities have offered to take a number of Polish girls into their schools. For those who are chosen to go, this is a great opportunity to study the English language.' I sighed and shuffled my feet. Nobody else moved. 'Now, I have asked you here because I want each of you to consider attending a boarding school, here in New Zealand, where you will have the chance of an excellent education.'

She paused and looked carefully at each one of us. I

looked down at the floor, wondering how she could suggest such a thing. The camp was our home in this strange country. None of us wanted to leave. The other girls whispered together.

'Please ask me if you have any questions,' Madame Swietlicka said kindly.

Danuta stood up. 'Please, madame,' she said, 'you have taught us to be the little soldiers of Poland. We want to stay here and be together.'

'Danuta,' Madame Swietlicka said, 'Europe is still fighting a terrible war and this is not the time to talk of returning to Poland. We are lucky to have been able to find refuge in New Zealand and there is much that you can learn.' Danuta sat down and started fiddling with her braids.

'Now, are there any more questions?' Madame Swietlicka asked. We were all silent. 'Well then, finish your tea. I would like you all to think about what I have said.'

Two days later I was summoned to see Madame Swietlicka once again. She was sitting in her room looking very stern.

'Well, Krystyna,' she said, 'you will be leaving on Thursday. Please make sure that you have your things ready.'

Tears came to my eyes. I wanted to tell her that I would not go. I wanted to say that being at the camp meant everything to me, that I wanted to stay here forever, but I bit my lip and stared straight ahead.

'Do you have any questions?' Madame Swietlicka asked gently. I shook my head. 'Then run outside and play.' She patted my shoulder. 'You had better say goodbye to your friends.'

I couldn't think, I couldn't feel anything. My life had been full of goodbyes, and now I was again being sent away. I wanted to stay at the camp with the Polish people I knew, with faces that had become familiar, with people who knew my name and who tucked me into bed at night. I loved my friends Jadwiga and Basia whose beds were beside mine in the long dormitory. We would lie awake at night looking out the window at the stars and whispering stories about things that we remembered from our childhood in Poland. Out there, I could not speak the language and no one could even spell my name. The camp was my home and my place of belonging, and now I had to take leave of it. I shut myself into my sorrow and cried in secret places where no one could find me. I longed for one of my friends to come running with the news that I did not have to leave the camp. I was tired of always having to move on and accustom myself to people and places that were new.

On departure day I got up before the bell, put on my khaki uniform, emptied my chest of drawers of my Red Cross cardigan, dress, and pile of stored crusts, and crept outside before my friends could wake. I hid in a field behind the camp, watching as the day started and my friends began another morning in this happy place. Then the army truck rolled in through the gates and I knew it was time to go. I swallowed my tears, brushed down my uniform and joined the other girls who were waiting in front of the camp office with their bundles beside them. Madame Swietlicka was there, straightening uniforms and talking to the New Zealand soldiers. She put out her arms to pull me close, kissing me on both cheeks.

'Goodbye Krystyna,' she said.

I said goodbye and scrambled up into the back of the truck with the other girls, trying to blink away the tears that were flooding my eyes. The tail-gate slammed and suddenly we were off, bumping along the Pahiatua Track and heading for the Palmerston North railway station.

# Chapter 7

Another train journey. The familiar clacking of the train's wheels on the track took us further and further away from Pahiatua Camp. The rhythm of the wheels reminded me of that first train journey, so long ago. I stared out the window as tears flooded my face and I remembered my mother, my aunt, my sister and my brother. I bit my lips and stared at the fields and trees, forcing the memories from my mind.

'Don't cry, Krystyna.' Danuta was sitting beside me, holding my hand. I put my head in her lap and shook with tears. '*Moja cochana*,' she whispered stroking my hair. 'Don't cry, little one.'

But I did. I cried until I was empty, glad of Danuta's closeness. When I sat up, her arm was still around me. The other girls were standing side by side with their heads poking out the window, their hair blown about by the wind from the train. They looked excited and happy. It was better to forget the other train where the tiny window near the roof was solidly barred.

The ticket collector began rattling his way through the carriage. 'Tickets please, tickets please,' he repeated in the same tone until he came to our seats. He reached over and tapped Zofia's shoulder. 'Excuse me, Miss,' he said.

Zofia pulled her head in through the window and stared at the man.

'Can't you read the sign?' he said. 'It is not permitted to put your head out the window ... otherwise ... *karoomph* ...' and he made a cutting-off gesture across his neck.

Danuta, Zofia and I laughed but we tugged Eva's coat and shut the window. We couldn't read the sign but none of us wanted to have our heads snapped off.

'That's better,' the conductor said, nodding approvingly at us. 'Have a toffee.' He held out a wrinkled brown bag and we helped ourselves to a sweet wrapped in paper.

'Thank you,' we said one after the other, stuffing our mouths with the sticky brown sweets.

'Now, what about tickets?' the man asked, putting the bag of sweets in his pocket and getting out a shiny metal clicker. Danuta held out our tickets and he punched a tiny piece out of them. 'The Polish girls, eh?' He gave us a long, steady look. 'I'll be back to let you know when we're getting close to Wellington.'

At the station we were met by a young woman wearing

a modern nipped-in-the-waist costume and shoes with very high heels.

'I'm Julie,' she said, kissing each of us on the cheek. 'Let's have a cuppa.' She led us to the station tearooms where we ate and drank until we were bursting. I wondered how the smart young woman managed to keep her waist so small. Then we walked to the South Island ferry wharf where Julie saw us safely up the ramp and gave each of us a shiny half-crown.

'Good luck,' she said and clip-clopped away on her high heels. We gazed after her, spellbound.

The ship's engines started up, the ropes were untied and the ferry whooshed out into the deep sea of Cook Strait. We stood on the deck, feeling the wind buffet our faces and watching the houses of Wellington disappear behind us. It was only two years since we had arrived in this place and gazed up at the houses on the hill, searching for one that might mean something special. They seemed familiar now, the land around them less foreign and frightening. It troubled me that I could hardly remember the house where I was born and the little bedroom with the carved bed that had once been mine. The pain of loss was as deep as ever, yet the faces and the memories that were dear to me were becoming blurred in my mind.

I was glad of the company of the other girls. We walked up and down the decks, holding hands and singing Polish songs into the raging wind. We leaned on the rails and wrote wishes which we dropped down into the sea, running to the back of the ship to try to see them disappearing in the wake. We sat on the lifeboat rafts and made plans for our future until a man with a beery breath came and sat beside us and asked us our names. Danuta shouted at him in Polish to leave us alone and he hurried back to the coziness of the bar. We slept the night in a little bunkroom deep inside the ship, comforted by our friendship as the ship ploughed southwards.

In the morning we were all rather subdued, even Danuta. We got dressed and went up on deck just as the ferry turned into Lyttelton Harbour. The bare hills closed in and we stared ahead, trying to glimpse the port. Waiting for us on the wharf were two nuns who were dressed from head to foot in swathes of black material. All we could see was the middle part of their faces and their hands as they reached out to pull us from the crowd of disembarking passengers.

'I'm Sister Agnes and this is Sister Annunciata,' the taller nun said.

'Good morning,' we chorused and curtsied.

The nuns hustled us along the wharf and on to a train, unhooking their rosary beads as soon as they sat down. We clustered together anxiously.

'Don't sit next to the window,' Sister Agnes said to Danuta. 'You'll get dirty hands.'

We were taken to Our Lady of Victories, a school for girls in Christchurch. The nuns led us in through the heavy front door and locked it behind us. There was a bench against the wall in the dark corridor.

'Sit down,' the nuns said. 'Wait here for the Reverend Mother.'

We sat in a row with our hands folded in our laps, watching the door. As the Reverend Mother entered we stood up and curtsied.

'Sit, girls,' she said. We sat. 'Now listen carefully.' The Reverend Mother spoke slowly. 'The school you are being sent to has a polio epidemic and is in quarantine. In the meantime you are to stay here with us. Do you understand me?'

We nodded our heads, though none of us was sure what she was saying. The Reverend Mother clapped her hands loudly. Immediately two girls wearing navy blue dresses appeared in the doorway.

'Take these Polish girls to the dormitory and show them their beds,' the Reverend Mother said.

'Yes, Mother.'

We curtsied and turned to leave.

'One last thing,' the Reverend Mother said, 'I will write and compliment your teachers on your lovely manners.'

'Thank you,' we replied and left the room, following the navy-blue girls down a highly polished dark corridor. All over the walls were pictures of people whose bodies were bleeding. They had crosses in their hands and circles of light over their heads but the sides of their bodies, their hands and their feet were pouring blood. These pictures and the habits that the nuns wore seemed severe and frightening.

The girls took us upstairs to a dormitory where there were rows and rows of beds with floral bedspreads. The whole place was swarming with girls and flowers. A nun was sitting at a table in the doorway and when she saw us she called four girls out of the busy room and asked them to help us unpack. I followed a short girl with curly black hair down the length of the dormitory. She pointed to an empty bed, grabbed my bundle and tossed it on to the bed. The string came off and out tumbled my raggy clothes. The girl burst out laughing.

'Hey, look at this!' she called, and girls in navy blue crowded around my pile of clothes. They held up my ragged knickers and giggled uproariously.

'Let's see what she's wearing now,' one of them suggested and flicked up my skirt. 'Whoopeee …' she cried, exposing my holey bloomers for the closest to see. I wrenched the edge of my skirt from her fingers and smoothed it back against my legs. Tears rushed to my eyes and I swallowed hard, trying not to cry. A nun appeared, walking towards us down the corridor of floral beds.

'Girls, girls,' she said, clapping her hands. 'Quieten down.' The girls scurried away and I was left standing beside my new bed, folding my tatty clothes.

'Goodness gracious me,' Sister said, stopping beside me. 'Those clothes are entirely unsuitable.'

I kept on folding. Tears were poking the backs of my eyes but I refused to cry. I put my dress and cardigan in the chest of drawers beside the bed and waited to be told what to do next.

We were summoned to the parlour, and there were introduced to six New Zealand ladies wearing hats and holding large handbags. We curtsied and said, 'Good morning.'

'Nice manners,' one of the ladies remarked.

We stood there while they talked about us. Four girls in a row, eyes down, staring at the floral pattern on the carpet. After a while the women freshened their lipstick and said that we had better be going to town.

'We'll need two cars,' one of them said. 'The Polish girls will take up the whole back seat.'

We drove into Christchurch around the edge of a large park where people were walking under the dappled shade of the trees. The women talked all the time about clothes and men and children. We Polish girls sat together in silence, listening, and I realised that most of the time I could work out what was being said, even when I didn't know all the words. For a minute or two I stopped being nervous: this was my secret key to the world where I felt so different.

We went shopping in a department store called Ballantyne's. I had never been to a place like it before. There were clothes hanging everywhere and shop assistants standing behind polished wooden counters. The women led the way upstairs to 'School Uniforms' where there were rows of clothes all coloured black or navy blue. A woman assistant emerged from among the racks.

'Ah … the Polish girls,' she said. 'Please come this way,' and she led us to a row of curtained cubicles.

'I'll mind them,' one of the women said. She pushed us into separate cubicles and then pulled the curtains. 'Clothes off!' she said, miming the action of pulling off her dress. I looked at her in horror.

'No!' I shouted wrapping my arms tightly around my body.

I didn't want anyone else to see my ragged underwear.

'Listen here, my lady,' the woman said, 'you do as I say.' And she stuck her face very close to mine and tweaked my ear.

'Oww!' I squealed, trying to wriggle away. The woman moved closer and stood on my toe, hard. I raised my arms and took off my dress, standing there in front of her in my tatty underwear.

'Everything,' the woman said, indicating my knickers. Reluctantly I pulled them off and stood there feeling shy and embarrassed, trying to cover my newly emerging breasts with my arms. There was a mirror facing me and I could see the woman staring at my naked body.

'Hmm,' she said, 'there's not much of you.'

I tried to stand straighter with my arms still wrapped tightly around my body.

'Hands by sides,' the woman said, showing me what she meant. I felt a deep blush burning my face as I slowly moved my hands to my sides. The woman stared at my tiny breasts. 'It's disgusting,' she said, 'the sooner we get you into a brassiere the better.'

The other women crowded the cubicle, bringing piles of fresh new clothes. I put on a bra which fastened with hooks across my back and made me feel as if I couldn't breathe properly. Over the bra went a singlet, then a blue blouse and a navy blue pleated gym frock which came to my calves. The women pulled and tucked and said that it was better to buy on the big side as I'd need plenty of room for growing. They gave me a pair of white bloomers and two scratchy brown

162

woollen stockings which were held up with something called a suspender belt, a strange-looking contraption made of bits of rubber and elastic that tied tightly around my middle. There was a navy blue school blazer which hung from my shoulders and a felt hat with a brim that turned up all around the sides. I felt like a stuffed animal with all these clothes on, and the new undergarments were tight and uncomfortable.

The women eyed each piece of clothing and discussed its quality.

'You're very lucky, you know,' one of them said, tugging at my gym frock. 'Fancy getting away with all this for nothing.'

All I wanted to do was run away from that soft closeted cubicle and rip off that brassiere and suspender belt. I didn't feel lucky. I felt as if I was being cut in two across the middle.

There was one woman who stood a little apart from the others and ignored all the pulling and poking. When the other women moved on to the next cubicle she came closer, smiling softly. 'I'm Mrs Wilding,' she said, touching me gently on the head with her gloved hand, 'but you must call me Monica.'

I looked up at her and was caught in a most beautiful smile.

She was wearing a hat that wreathed the top half of her face and her brown eyes twinkled from below the rim.

'What about a Sunday dress for these girls?' she asked the other women as they clustered around outside our cubicles. 'Look here, its not a free-for-all,' said the woman who had told me to take my clothes off. 'Besides, what's wrong with them wearing their uniforms on Sundays?'

'They'll be the only ones in uniform,' Monica said, 'and the school regulations say that the girls need one informal dress for Sundays.'

'I won't stand for it,' said one of the others, harumphing heavily. 'We don't want them getting ideas above their station. They'll be cooks and kitchen maids … that's where they're going. No point wasting public money on Sunday dresses.'

Then the three other girls emerged from their cubicles, and I stopped listening to the women. I just hoped that I didn't look as strange as they did. Danuta's blouse was gaping at her neck and her gym frock was so long it brushed the floor. I swallowed hard, trying to stifle the giggles that rose in my throat. Although these clothes were all crisp and new, we still looked like the recipients of a Red Cross parcel.

I felt Monica's soft hand on my head as she continued talking to the other women. 'Look,' she said, with her eyes flashing under the brim of her hat, 'I don't give a damn about public money. They're going to have summer dresses,' and pulling me along by the arm she swept out of 'School Uniforms'. Danuta tripped over her gym frock trying to keep up with us.

Monica led the four of us downstairs to 'Day Dresses' where she pointed to several racks of pretty light-coloured dresses and suggested that we each choose one that we liked. For a minute or two we hesitated, thinking that perhaps we had misunderstood what she'd asked.

'Go on, then,' Monica said, sitting back on a stool beside the counter and lighting a cigarette.

Danuta was the first to start looking through the rows of clothes. Flashes of pink, mauve, yellow and green were waved past my face. Soon she had chosen a beautiful iris-blue dress with a white lace collar.

'Slip it on,' Monica urged, indicating the dressing rooms in the corner.

Danuta emerged transformed. Gone was the solemn-faced Polish refugee who cried under the blankets at night. In her new dress, Danuta looked like a princess. I rushed to the racks, searching for the one that would be mine.

We had a friend for life in Monica, and because she was the wife of old Harry Wilding who was as rich as the Rural Bank, Monica was used to getting her own way. She paid for the Sunday dresses with a cheque and then took us to afternoon tea, piling our plates with brandy snaps and lamingtons. While we ate she smoked cigarettes and drank coffee. I thought that she was the most beautiful woman I had ever seen.

The school in Christchurch became our home for a time, and every day we worked in the kitchen, scrubbing the pots, peeling potatoes and polishing floors. We joined the rest of the girls for Religious Instruction and had our meals in the school dining room, although we had to sit at different tables from one another so that we would not speak Polish. That was strictly forbidden. My hands were puffy and swollen from spending hours in soapy water and my back was sore. I longed to be able to speak to Danuta and the others. Sometimes we managed to sneak a few whispered words together, but we felt awkward and guilty. Polish seemed like part of a world that was lost to us now.

One afternoon I glanced up from scouring the floor to see Monica delicately stepping over the wet linoleum.

'Hello, darlings,' she said. 'I'm taking you out.' She lit a cigarette and sent us upstairs to change into our Sunday dresses. Transformed from kitchen maids into young women, we climbed into the green Armstrong Siddeley that was parked outside the convent's front door, while Monica left an explanatory note in the Reverend Mother's office. Then we drove up the Cashmere Hills to the Sign of the Kiwi where Monica led us up a winding path to the tea house overlooking the Canterbury Plains. She ordered Devonshire teas, custard squares and ice cream for us while she drank black coffee. Monica seemed like an old friend and our English had improved dramatically, so it was easy to answer her endless questions about our school days.

'You must stick up for yourselves,' she told us. 'Be proud and strong.' And then she started telling us about the ball she'd been to where she danced with the Archbishop so often that her husband was jealous. 'Just like a man,' she said, neatly tapping ash from her cigarette into the ashtray.

We nodded and smiled with our mouths full of pastry. It was heaven sitting up there in the clouds, looking down at the Canterbury Plains sprawling below us. Monica leaned towards us and stubbed out her last cigarette.

'Now listen, kids,' she said, 'don't let things get you down. This is a great little country.'

We smiled and wiped the flakes of pastry from the corners of our mouths. Monica took our photographs in the rock garden before we climbed back into the car and drove to school. 'See you later,' she said, blowing us kisses.

I stood watching while she roared away, feeling more alone than ever. Monica had seemed to understand how funny if felt to be different from the other girls. Being with her made it easier to see the right thing to do, simply because she didn't make me feel as if everything I did was strange or wrong.

Our days passed in a blur of cleaning and scrubbing until one morning the Reverend Mother summoned us to the front parlour where she announced that the quarantine had ended. We were to leave for Timaru on the first bus in the morning. The dormitory sister gave each of us a suitcase for our new clothes. Mine had LMC stamped in gold on the side. The girl who slept in the bed beside me said that it had belonged to one of the young women who had just entered the convent. Her name was Louise Mary Clark. I packed Louise's suitcase and folded the sheets and blankets on my dormitory bed. Sister Imelda went with us to the bus depot and made the sign of the cross on our foreheads. 'God go with you, my children,' she said.

The land was flat as we drove out of Christchurch, the plains stretching for miles towards the distant mountains. We drove on and on, stopping at two or three tiny towns where the driver offloaded bags of mail and other packages. The four of us were quiet, and a little apprehensive. None of us knew what awaited us at our new school — would we be allowed to speak Polish there? The bus ground on through the outlying districts of Timaru and we glimpsed the Pacific Ocean crashing against the shores of the town. As we climbed down from the bus I sniffed the strong salty smell of the sea. A nun was waiting for us outside the depot. She motioned to us to collect our suitcases and follow her. At the corner of the street she opened the back door of a car parked at the side of the road. Sitting behind the wheel was an elderly man with a brown weathered face. He turned and smiled as Danuta scrambled in.

'Mr Shanahan, these are the Polish girls,' the nun said. The man nodded and smiled. 'Bags in the boot,' he said with a jerk of his head.

The nun pointed us to the back of the car where we heaved open the boot and put our cases inside. As soon as we let go, the boot dropped with a clang.

'Steady on …' Mr Shanahan shouted out the window.

I swallowed hard and climbed inside the car, followed by Eva and Zofia. No one said a word as we drove to the Timaru convent, although Mr Shanahan whistled a tune through the front of his teeth.

At first sight the Timaru convent reminded me of Poland. It was a grand, grey stone building, three or four storeys high, with rows of tiny windows looking out on to the garden below. The grounds were leafy and green with huge trees and spacious shady lawns which shimmered like green velvet. As we drove closer I could see dozens of girls standing in lines in front of the steps to the main entrance of the building. They stared as the car came to a halt. Mr Shanahan climbed out to hold the door open for the nun. We scrambled out after her and found ourselves face to face with girls in navy blue tunics like ours.

'These are the Polish girls,' the nun announced.

We stared at the girls who were staring at us.

'*Dzien dobri*,' Danuta said, but her voice was shaky. A ripple of laughter rang through the girls who were looking so hard at us.

'Come along,' said the nun, and she made a sharp clicking noise with something in her pocket.

Immediately the girls in rows turned and began to file, two by two, into the stone building. Danuta, Eva, Zofia and I followed along behind them. It was dark inside and very cool. We walked along a corridor with our footsteps echoing loudly. The nun paused outside a heavy door and tapped lightly.

'Enter!' a voice called.

The nun opened the door and pushed us inside. 'The Reverend Mother,' she whispered and shut the door behind us.

It was dark in that room and smelt faintly of furniture wax and roses. The windows were heavily curtained and there was a huge crucifix on the wall.

'Welcome, girls,' said a voice from the depths of the shadows. We turned to look in its direction. The Reverend Mother was sitting behind a highly polished desk, bare except for a crucifix in front of her. We curtsied, a wavering line of four girls. The Reverend Mother looked at each of us very carefully. You could feel her eyes on you, poking and prying into the corners of your soul.

'We must pray together, girls,' she said, closing her eyes and folding her hands. We knelt on the floor in front of the desk while the Reverend Mother thanked God for our deliverance and asked His will to guide us. After the 'Amen' she glided out from behind the desk and touched each of us lightly on the head.

'I want you to treat this convent as your home,' she said, 'and I expect you to act accordingly.' She seemed to expect some sort of reply, so we all curtsied again, inclining our heads towards the crucifix behind her on the wall. Then she indicated a bench along the back wall. We sat in a row and waited. Finally she spoke again. 'I am sure that you will be happy with us. I have, however, taken steps to separate you from each other and you will not be permitted to talk in Polish among yourselves.'

Danuta sighed and shuffled her feet while I stared at my hands clasped together in my lap.

'You are here to learn English,' the Reverend Mother said. 'Please remember that … and as your education is free I expect you to contribute to the daily running of our community.' Then she rang a little bell by the doorway. Almost immediately a nun appeared at the open door. 'Sister,' the Reverend Mother said, 'take the Polish girls to the bathroom and attend to their hair.' She tapped Danuta on the shoulder and the rest of us hurried to our feet. 'God go with you,' the Reverend Mother said, sitting back behind her desk. We curtsied and moved towards the door. 'Girls,' she called, 'it is not necessary to curtsey.' She rang another little bell and the nun closed the door.

Once again we were walking down the long dark corridor with our footsteps echoing behind us. Somewhere on the left the nun pushed open a heavy wooden door and we walked into a huge bathroom with white tiles on three sides. Along the other wall stretched a long mirror that was speckled with green mould.

'Wait here,' the nun said and left the bathroom.

We stood and looked at ourselves in the mirror. Four serious reflections stared back. No one spoke and no one smiled. In two or three minutes the nun was back carrying a stool and a large pair of scissors.

'You first,' she said, pointing to Eva.

I caught my breath as the nun began to cut away Eva's curls. It had taken so long for us to grow our hair since it was shaved in Teheran. I closed my eyes while the nun snipped Eva's hair, then I felt her hand on my shoulder. 'You next,' she said, and I took three slow steps to the stool and sat down. As soon as the scissors began cutting away my hair I started crying. I stuffed my fist into my mouth but tears poured down my face. 'Sit still,' the nun said irritably, jabbing the scissors into my neck. I tried to sit still but I couldn't stop crying, weeping for the loss of my hair, my home and the warmth of my mother's arms.

Slowly we got used to the routines that regularised life at the Timaru convent school. It seemed to be an enormous place with more than four hundred boarders, among whom 'the Polish girls' made a huge impression. Everyone wanted to look at us. During school assembly we had to stand in the front, below the stage, where hundreds of faces stared back at us.

This was the only time we were together. During the school day we were in different rooms and different classes. The Sister gave me a seat at the front of the classroom and I tried to follow the lessons, reading from books in which the only words I knew were 'at' and 'the'. The class was conducted at Form Three level, but without any knowledge of English I was dumb. There were so many things I wanted to know, but I did not have the English words to ask with. At recess I huddled alone on the edge of the playground, hoping for a glimpse of my Polish friends. Sometimes I saw them, alone like me, and we smiled and waved. Sometimes I was approached by two or three of the New Zealand girls who encouraged me to join their circle. For a while my nervousness thawed, but they asked such strange questions, like 'Do you have bread in Poland?' that I felt silly. My face would be red and embarrassed and my mouth dry. I felt sure there was something not quite right about me, something to do with being Polish.

The Reverend Mother had allotted each of us a number of household duties. Every morning we rose an hour earlier than the other girls in order to do the work that earned our keep. Eva cleaned the toilets, Danuta scrubbed the white-tiled bathroom and Zofia polished the floors of the long dark corridors. I worked in the laundry, boiling the copper and turning the mangle to wring out the heavy towels and sheets. It was here that I practised my English, which remained slow and hesitant despite the daily lessons, for I was too scared to speak in front of the others in my class in case the words came out wrong. For weeks I sat in the front row, turning the pages of the books I could not read, trying to make sense of the unfamiliar words. Eventually the Reverend Mother sent me to the infants' classroom where I perched at the back on a tiny chair and listened to five-year-olds stammering out their lessons. I had a reading book about Janet and John and another book that was full of multiplication tables. I made lists of words in my head and memorised them, trying to work out what they meant. Gradually I was able to put together words and phrases, hardly daring to use them in case the other girls laughed when I spoke. My voice was strange and seemed unable to master the patter of English as spoken by the other girls. After a while I was permitted to re-join the Form Three class where the chairs were normal sized and things improved, except for the problem of always being different. Whenever there was a parents' day or Mass at the Timaru Cathedral people stared and pointed us out. It was like being part of a four-girl zoo. I got sick of being watched. I wanted to be like the other girls in my class who were so plump and pretty and whose parents sent them food parcels and jars of raspberry jam.

Spring came and early summer. Near the end of the school year the Reverend Mother summoned us to her office.

'Girls,' she said, 'out of Christian kindness a number of parents have offered to take you into their homes over the school holidays.'

'But Reverend Mother,' Danuta protested, speaking slowly and carefully. 'I thought that we would be returning to Pahiatua Camp.'

'I am doing what is best for you,' the Reverend Mother said. She rang the little bell and another nun came to the door. 'The Polish girls are to pack their cases,' she ordered. That was the end of the matter.

I went to stay with the Dendrons in Fairlie. Joe Dendron was the fat friendly engine driver on the 'Fairlie Flyer'. His daughter Moira was one of the most popular girls in Form Five. She was the best typist and Miss Hight who taught Commercial said that Moira had a good future ahead of her.

Moira and her buddies really whooped it up on the train trip home to Fairlie. They climbed aboard laden with bags of licorice allsorts, oddfellows and toffees. They bought bottles of pop with the caps off and stowed them carefully in the luggage rack. At Pleasant Point they rushed out and bought ham sandwiches and ice creams. It was hard to get used to being surrounded by food. I still remembered the time when there was nothing to eat and my stomach was twisted with the pain. I always had a little piece of bread in the bottom of my pocket in case there was a time when the emptiness would come back. I looked at the lollies that the girls gobbled up one after the other, and craved that sweet taste in my mouth. I fingered the bread in my pocket. Bread had once meant everything to me, but now I couldn't stop myself wanting sweets and coloured soft drink like the other girls had. Moira was kind and offered me sweets, even though she only knew me as 'one of the Polish girls'. We didn't talk much. I sat and looked out the window with my mouth full, staring out at the wide fields which were burnt golden in the hot summer sun.

There was a great turnout at the Fairlie station where everybody hugged and kissed Moira and said that she looked beaut. I stood on the edge of the platform, uncertain how to introduce myself. Then Moira's mum pushed her way through and hugged me. 'Gidday, dearie,' she said, clasping me to her bosom. 'You'll be right at home with us, you'll see.' And she grabbed me by the hand and dragged me into the middle of the crowd, shouting my name above the din as she introduced me to friends and relations.

Moira's dad, Joe, was on duty, but there seemed to be five or six willing men on the platform who loaded our bags up into the back of the Works truck and helped Moira, Mrs Dendron and me up into the cab. I sat by the window with my arm stuck out while Moira, who was squashed in the middle, chatted away to the driver.

'That's Barney,' Mrs Dendron said, digging me in the ribs.

I blushed and looked away. I'd heard Moira talking about Barney in the dormitory at night and I knew that she was planning to get around with him all summer. Moira reckoned that he was one of the best kissers around but all I could see was his hairy leg on the clutch pedal and a huge hand that slammed the truck into gear.

The Dendrons lived in a railway house beside the railway line in Fairlie. Barney drove us right to the front door and then unloaded our suitcases and carried them inside. Moira lingered by the back of the truck and Mrs Dendron took my hand.

'Come along, dearie,' she said. 'Let's boil the billy.'

We walked up the grey concrete path along the side of the house. Mrs Dendron showed me the last of the gladioli and the first of the phlox. 'I'm not much in the garden,' she said, huffing as she heaved herself down to pull out a bit of twitch. 'I never got the hang of those green fingers but I always feed the gladys with cold tea.'

Inside, the house was warm and smelled of coal dust. Mrs Dendron filled the kettle and placed it on the coal range. 'She's a beauty,' Mrs Dendron said as I watched her stoke and poke the embers. 'We've always got more than enough hot water and it keeps the whole place toasty.' She bustled around the kitchen, opening cake tins and putting cups and saucers on the table.

'Is there ... anything I can do?' I asked, still standing awkwardly by the range.

'Oohh, you're a good girlie,' Mrs Dendron said. 'As soon as we've had a cuppa I'll get you on to peeling the potatoes.'

We sat down to eat cakes and drink tea that tasted strong and tarry. Soon Moira burst in through the back door and started pushing pikelets into her flushed cheeks.

'That's my girl,' Mrs Dendron said admiringly. 'I made a double batch this morning,' and she urged me to have another one.

We ate and drank until the teapot was empty and our stomachs full. Mrs Dendron took out her knitting.

'It's a layette,' she told me when I sat down beside her and fingered the wool. I hadn't heard that word before and I tucked it away in the back of my head. 'Do you know how to knit, Christine?' I shook my head. 'Well, tomorrow morning we'll get you started,' she said.

I liked being part of the Dendron family. It was a long time since I had been in a home, and just being in a place where there were four chairs and a table gave me a warm, comfortable sort of feeling. At night Moira and I shared the softest bed I had ever slept on and Mrs Dendron tucked us in, piling up the thick scratchy woollen blankets until I felt as if I was being buried alive. Moira went straight to sleep after drawing an imaginary line down the bed across which I was not allowed to sprawl.

'I don't mind you, kiddo,' she said, 'but I don't like being crowded. And after all, it is my bed.'

I hung on to the edge of the mattress and tried not to turn over, worried that I would not be able to sleep. But when I opened my eyes Mrs Dendron was pulling back the heavy blue curtains.

'Wake up, sleepy heads,' she said and a train went thundering past.

That day was like all the others. Every morning around eleven Mrs Dendron would bring us breakfast in bed, staggering in with a tray piled high with food. Fried eggs, sausages, liver and bacon, and piles of toast and homemade raspberry jam. We sat up and ate until we were bursting and then Moira would jump out of bed and make for the bathroom. Mrs Dendron was busy doing the housework with the windows wide open and the National Programme on the radio. After half an hour or so Moira would emerge looking fresh and clean except for her face which was covered in a chalky white layer of powder. 'My make-up,' she called it. I scuttled into the bathroom after her and scrubbed my face and hands. In the mirror over the basin an unfamiliar girl looked back at me. I seemed to be growing, and there were hairs sprouting under my arms. I quickly pulled on my Sunday dress. It was the only thing I had to wear besides my school uniform and Moira had made it perfectly clear that you don't wear your school uniform while you're on holiday.

One morning Moira didn't wait for her mother to bring our breakfast in bed. She was up early, organising a bike ride to Strathmore Corner, five or six miles down the main road. I made the bed and went to the kitchen where Moira's enthusiasm had turned the place upside down.

'You'll be on, won't you Christine?' Moira said as soon as she saw me. 'It'll be a good chance to have a look around.' I smiled and got on with the dishes. I didn't want to tell her that I couldn't ride a bike.

Moira and her mum threw themselves into the idea of an excursion. They put the word around Fairlie, borrowing bikes here and there so that there would be enough for five or six of Moira's special friends and me. Several of them actually had bikes of their own, smart sports bikes with tartan covers over the back spokes to keep the mud off the hem of your dress. I, meanwhile, was put in charge of making the sandwiches. 'Meat and pickle, cheese, onion and egg,' Mrs Dendron instructed me. 'And don't forget to spread the butter properly.'

I stood at the wooden bench buttering slice after slice. Then I piled them together with the fillings; the meat kept slipping sideways and the onion made my eyes water. There was a knot of dread in the bottom of my stomach. Soon the sandwiches would be made and we'd have to go. Everyone would see that I didn't know how to ride a bike.

I took a break from the sandwiches, rinsing my hands in the sink and covering the piles of food with a damp tea towel, the way that Mrs Dendron had taught me. Then I went outside and sat on the back doorstep, wondering if I could learn to ride a bike without anyone knowing. I was sure there couldn't be all that much to it. I'd seen Moira sailing up and down the street on hers, her skirt billowing out behind her. Then I saw it, a borrowed bike leaning up against the woodshed. Looking around to make sure no one was about, I grabbed the bike and jumped on, pumping the pedals as hard as I could. Crash! I smacked to the ground, ending up in a tangle of twisted bike with my dress wedged in the oily chain. I wrenched it free but the material made a tearing noise and the skirt came away stained with thick black oil. I righted the bike and jumped on again, but I was scared and panicky. Any minute Moira or her mum might turn up. I tucked my dress into my knickers and wobbled around the backyard, trying to keep my balance, but it was no good. I smacked to the ground again, grazing my leg.

Before anyone could see me, I propped the bike up against the woodshed and scuttled inside to make some more sandwiches, hoping that no one would notice the oil stains on my dress.

Moira and her mother came in, laughing victoriously. They had organised six bikes and borrowed a parka for me in case it rained. I propped myself against the bench and buttered more bread. My stomach churned with dread.

'Are you all right, Christine?' Moira's mother asked. I nodded and then shook my head, confused about how to answer. Mrs Dendron put her broad hand across my forehead. 'Jeepers,' she said, 'this kid's got a temperature. No biking for you, young lady. It's straight to bed.' And she took the bread knife from my hand and gave me a gentle push towards the bedroom. I sat on the pile of soft eiderdowns, took off my socks and shoes and climbed into the big soft bed, crying with relief at having escaped the bike ride. Mrs Dendron pulled the curtains and brought me a cup of tea.

'Just lie there, dearie,' she said. 'Don't fret, you'll be able to go biking another day.'

I was still in bed when Moira and her friends came home. They crowded into the bedroom and Moira presented me with a big bunch of dandelions.

Mrs Dendron cleared them out of the bedroom smartly. 'Tea's ready,' she said, waving her apron at Moira's friends. 'And I don't want you disturbing poor Christine. I don't know what the nuns would say if I sent her back with a cold in the head.'

I went back to school feeling determined. I needed to

make myself understood in English. All day I practised English words and phrases in my head. I asked the nuns for books so that I could practise my reading. They gave me a copy of Oliver Twist and I read it slowly with a dictionary beside me, but when I got to the end the only thing I knew about the story was that Oliver was a boy. I asked for another book and they gave me Wuthering Heights. I read and read because I wanted to be able to think in English without first having to change the words from Polish to English in my head.

Mrs Dendron didn't forget about me. She always included something for me in Moira's food parcels. I wrote to her every two or three weeks, practising my English, though she never replied. It was good to have someone to write to, even if she was another girl's mother.

The August school holidays seemed to come around very quickly. This time the Reverend Mother summoned us to her office and said that we were permitted to visit Pahiatua Camp. 'I am pleased with your progress in English,' she said. 'Please do not revert to speaking Polish while you are away.'

Her news was wonderfully exciting. The four of us joined hands as we walked back down the corridor, hardly able to believe our luck. Danuta said that she hated this place and that she would never return.

'But what will you do?' I asked her.

'I don't know,' she said. 'Get married and go to work. I just don't want to spend any more time in this place where I'm never any good at anything.' That night she crept across the dormitory to my bed and by the light of a candle showed me the big bundle of letters that she had received from Stas, one of the boys at the camp.

'He puts Madame Swietlicka's name on the outside of the envelope,' she said. 'That way they get past the Reverend Mother unopened.'

I handled her bundle of letters reverently. Danuta and Stas seemed destined to share a future together. I wondered what would happen to me.

Our return to Pahiatua Camp was like a home-coming. The same army trucks picked us up at the station and drove us along the Pahiatua Track. This time the fields seemed familiar and the bends in the road were like welcoming friends. At the camp everyone was assembled to greet us with hugs and kisses, singing and dancing, and best of all with flowing words of Polish. We were escorted to the dining room where a feast had been laid on the tables. The army cooks had been replaced by Poles and we sat down to *ogourki* and *piroshki*, *cernik* and *markowicz*, food that we had not tasted since leaving Poland. It was a relief not to have to think every word in your head before you spoke it. We talked and laughed and sometimes we cried but we knew that we had come home to a place where we could be Polish.

After a few days Madame Swietlicka invited us to her house. We ate tea and cakes, but without the same nervousness that we had once felt at being in her home. We talked about school and showed off our English. Danuta spoke last, asking if she would be permitted to leave school and go to work.

'Well ...' Madame Swietlicka spoke slowly. 'I think it is time for the five of us to talk about the future and about what is going to happen to you girls.' Madame Swietlicka refilled her cup and sighed. We knew that the war had ended. Now she told us that our country was dominated by the Soviet Union. The Poland that we had left as children no longer existed. Those who had a living relative in Poland were welcome to return, but the rest of us were offered a home in New Zealand.

'We are lucky to be allowed to stay in this country,' Madame Swietlicka said with tears running down her face. 'We will always be Polish but now most of us will be Polish New Zealanders.'

The news came as a shock. We had never thought that we might not be able to return to Poland. It was our homeland and our life, the language and country that we knew. That night we sat on our beds in the dormitories, talking urgently. Tears were never far from our eyes as we tried to work out what would happen to us now. Danuta was there, with Stas beside her. I knew that they would help each other to stay Polish, and in a way I envied their love. I had no life outside the school and the Pahiatua Camp. I had no family that I knew of in Poland. I had no one.

I plunged myself into camp activities, clinging to the people and the place where I felt most at home. Being free to speak in Polish, to sing Polish songs and to attend Mass in my own language all seemed more important than ever.

Here I could forget about the awkwardness and uncertainty that I felt at school, and my new knowledge of English was even useful. Strangely, as I spent the mornings helping the younger children with their Polish lessons, English words kept popping up in my head. I felt as if I had begun a long journey from Polish to English, striving to perfect the new language, but unwilling to leave my Polishness behind.

Madame Swietlicka sent a message that she wanted to speak with me. She was alone in her house when I knocked at the door and she took me in her arms and held me tightly. 'Krysia,' she said, 'my little Krystyna.'

I stood rigid in her embrace, afraid that I would start weeping and never stop. We sat together hand in hand while Madame Swietlicka talked about the good report that the nuns had written about me. She praised me for being quick and eager to learn.

'You must carry on, Krysia,' she said, patting my hand. 'Lead the way so that the rest of our children will follow. You must study hard so that you will succeed here in New Zealand.'

I looked into her eyes and sighed. I felt scared and lonely. 'But what will happen?' I asked her. 'Where will we go?'

'The camp will soon disband,' Madame Swietlicka said. 'All the children will be sent to New Zealand schools and those who are old enough will go to work. We are going to establish two hostels in Wellington and one in Auckland so that there will be somewhere for you to come in the holidays. Now please pull yourself together and be a good example to the others.'

She kissed me on the head, handed me a handkerchief and sent me outside. For a long time I wandered around the camp, crying for my lost past and from fear of the unknown future before me. The camp had been something to belong to and now there was nothing.

I went back to school at Timaru full of dread, but I studied hard and succeeded. Soon the nuns were holding me up as an example to the other girls.

'Look at Christine,' they said. 'She came here without a word of English and now she is doing very well.'

That sort of praise didn't earn me any friends. I was always left out and lonely. Moira Dendron had left school and got a job as a secretary. There was no one else who had taken me up as a buddy. I tried to get on with the other girls but they all said that I spoke funny. Eva and Zofia made friends because they were good at sports, but although I tried I was hopeless at basketball and couldn't run fast enough to play hockey. I spent most of my spare time reading in the school library. I knew that soon I would have to leave school and that knowledge filled me with terror.

The summer holidays turned up again. Mrs Dendron had written asking if I would like to come down to Fairlie. I was looking forward to spending the hot summer months swimming in the river and walking through the fields. Maybe I would get the chance to learn how to ride a bicycle. The Reverend Mother summoned me to her office. Alone.

'Christine,' she said, 'the Shanahans need some help with Nan. Mrs Shanahan is not very well. I am sending you to them for the holiday period.'

'But Reverend Mother,' I begged, 'I am going to Fairlie to stay with the Dendrons.'

'You will go where I send you,' the Reverend Mother said. 'You must be grateful for a chance to help other people when you have been given so much.'

I pressed my lips tightly together. Any minute I would start crying. I waited until the Reverend Mother had dismissed me, then ran down the dark corridor, oblivious to the rules about walking quietly. There was nowhere private to go, except the toilets. I locked the door and leaned against it, crying and crying, pulling out handfuls of toilet paper and stuffing them into my mouth so that no one would hear. I had so wanted to go back to the Dendrons and the warm, homely routine of their life. I was tired of having to be grateful for whatever happened to me in New Zealand.

# Chapter 8

The Reverend Mother's decision seemed unfair. I was always getting used to people and then never seeing them again. This would be my third New Zealand family. The only thing I knew about the Shanahans was that Mr Shanahan was the school handyman and the girls used to laugh at his faded baggy overalls and down-at-heel shoes. It was Mr Shanahan who had picked us up at the railway station when we first arrived in Timaru and I could still remember the way he whistled through the front of his teeth.

On break-up day I packed my LMC suitcase and made my bed without sheets or pillowslip. The long dormitory had already emptied and the beds stood in long lifeless rows. The other girls were excitedly waiting downstairs, watching the cars arrive and looking out for their parents. I joined the crowd and waited at the back with my suitcase at my feet, watching as my classmates greeted their mothers and fathers and climbed gaily into the back of their cars. Down the end of the drive I glimpsed Mr Shanahan in the brown Vauxhall. I took a deep breath and picked up my bag.

'What's Shan up to?' one of the girls asked.

I felt myself blushing. The others stared down the driveway, watching as Mr Shanahan fiddled with the boot of the car and propped it open with a stick. 'First stop Reservoir Asylum ...' someone said, and the rest of her sentence was drowned in shrieks of laughter. I stood stiffly, unable to peel myself off from the girls' giggling. I knew that once I joined Mr Shanahan they'd start laughing at me too. The arriving parents were forgotten for a few minutes as everyone pushed and shoved, trying to get a better look at the caretaker. They stared while he re-lit his cigarette, and collapsed in laughter as he hitched up his saddle tweeds.

'Now then, girls ...' said a voice behind us. 'What is the cause of all this hilarity?' Sister Immaculata stood at the bottom of the stairs with her arms folded. Silence settled. She glared at us. 'I expect you to behave like young ladies. The noise I heard was like a tramstop on Friday night.' The faces stared at the ground. 'And you, Christine,' Sister Immaculata continued sharply. 'Run along, and don't keep Mr Shanahan waiting.' A muted murmur of giggling rippled through the crowd. 'Silence!' Sister said.

I picked up my suitcase and walked slowly towards the

car feeling thirty or forty pairs of eyes on my back.

'Gidday there,' Mr Shanahan said as he grabbed my case and threw it into the boot. I stood by the car feeling hot and embarrassed, unsure whether to climb in. Fortunately, just then Maud Aiken's mother drove up in a brand new Chevrolet and she became the new centre of attention. Mr Shanahan stubbed out his cigarette on the sole of his boot and opened the car door. 'Jump in, m'dear', he said, slamming the door after me. We drove into town in silence, and Mr Shanahan parked the car in the main street.

'I'll be back in a tick,' he called, opening the door. 'Just pick up a few bits and pieces.'

I sat in the car and watched people walking up and down the street. There were girls from school among them and I envied their comfortableness, wondering how long it would be before I could walk up the street without being pointed out as 'the Polish girl'. Mr Shanahan came back with an armful of paper bags.

'Here we are,' he said, putting two bags in my lap. 'Tucker time.'

A delicious smell filled the car. Mr Shanahan started up the engine and opened one of his bags. He steered the car through the traffic with one hand and munched on the pie he held in the other. I opened my bag and began to eat, even though I didn't feel hungry. My first bite of the crisp pastry and the rich gravy inside made my toes wiggle with joy. Food was still a preoccupation for me, and I often found myself eating just because I couldn't turn away an offer of food. At school there were often second helpings of shepherd's pie and silverbeet and I always held out my plate, even when I felt full. Food made me feel safe, and even now, sitting in Mr Shanahan's car with my mouth full of pie, life suddenly seemed to be full of promise. We finished the pies and brushed the crumbs off our laps on to the floor. Mr Shanahan pointed to the other bag. Inside was a soft cake covered with pink icing and coconut. 'Lamington,' Mr Shanahan said as he saw me examining it. I repeated the word after him and bit into the cake. It was sticky, sweet and soft in the middle, unlike anything I had tasted before. I ate it slowly, remembering the yeast cakes that my mother had made in Poland. The heavy smell of yeast baking filled the house and the cakes had a spongy freshness to them that was so different from the soft sweetness of this New Zealand cake.

Mr Shanahan ate his lamington in two bites. Then he crumpled his bag on to the floor and started singing. I sat listening, looking quickly at him from time to time because I had never seen a New Zealand man singing before. It was a rollicking, rolling sort of tune and in between the songs he talked to me about Queenie.

'Who is Queenie?' I asked after a while.

'The best heading dog in Southland,' Mr Shanahan said. 'You'll get to know her after a while.'

We drove into the full sun, with the light in our eyes. 'It's beautiful country,' Mr Shanahan said. 'Just beautiful.'

The food and the warmth of the sun made me feel relaxed.

I sat listening to Mr Shanahan's stories without

worrying what would happen once we arrived at Reservoir Cottage.

'Can you whistle, Christine?' he asked, pursing his lips and warbling like a bird.

'My name is Krystyna,' I told him and quickly stopped my mouth with my hand because I never mentioned my Polish name to anyone.

'Krystyna,' Mr Shanahan said thoughtfully. 'That's a pretty name. Got a good ring to it.'

I blushed and looked out the window. I was used to being called Christine here in New Zealand, but it felt as if I was losing part of myself, the part that was Polish.

'Would you get the gate?' Mr Shanahan asked as we turned off the road at Reservoir Hill. I climbed out of the car. The smell of summer was heavy in the air and heat shimmered above the dust from the road. The gate was latched with a heavy metal chain but I managed to open it and the Vauxhall chugged through. 'Good on you, girlie,' Mr Shanahan said as he put the car in second. 'It's pretty steep all the way up from here.'

At first sight Reservoir Cottage reminded me of Poland, the way it nestled among trees with wide fields all around. It was a small house with a green tin roof and a flower garden that came right up to the front door of the house. The colours were strong and vivid. Red, pink, purple, yellow and blue flowers nestled together like a huge multi-coloured bouquet. The air was dusky with their scent and a deep stillness settled around us.

'Here we are, home sweet home,' Mr Shanahan said as

he stopped the car. In the distance I could hear a dog barking. A woman appeared in the doorway, waving. Mr Shanahan waved back. 'That's Nan,' he said. 'She's a mongol.'

We unloaded my case from the back of the car and I followed Mr Shanahan up the path, sniffing the strong sweet smell of summer flowers. Nan walked down the path to meet us, holding out her hands in welcome and making soft cooing noises in the back of her throat. I stood back behind Mr Shanahan, unsure of what to say.

'Nan, this is Krystyna,' Mr Shanahan said. 'She has come to stay with us for a while.'

Nan pushed past her father and stood looking at me. I stared back. She had a rather large round face and her eyes were very close together. Her nose was quite flat in the middle and she was short and stout as if she had been squashed together.

'Hello Krys … tyn … a,' Nan said.

'Hello Nan,' I replied and she smiled at me. It was a large, rather odd smile that sat heavily on her face.

'You'll have a friend for life in Nan,' Mr Shanahan said. 'Now let's go in and have a cuppa.'

I followed the others inside the house, where everything seemed clean, crisp and white. There was a starched cloth on the table which was set with cups and saucers ready for afternoon tea. Mr Shanahan tapped my shoulder.

'Come through here to your room,' he said, opening a door. 'And when you've finished unpacking I'll take you along to meet Marj.'

I couldn't believe that this was a room just for me. It was small and pretty, with bunches of flowers all over the wallpaper and pink curtains in the window. There was only one bed in the room, covered with a white tasseled bedspread. I put my case on the bed and sat down beside it. Tears flooded my eyes, but I was crying because I was so happy in that little bedroom with clumps of yellow and white flowers growing right outside the window. It was the first time since I had been a child in Poland that I would sleep in a room by myself. I was used to dormitory sleeping now, where my bed was one in a long row and nothing was private. I had learned to wait until lights were out before I let myself think about the life I was living. The rest of the time I was always being careful to try to do the right thing so that I would not stand out as one of the Polish girls. Alone in my room at Reservoir Cottage, I twirled around with joy and plumped down on the bed to test its softness. Through the wall I could hear Nan and Mr Shanahan talking to each other and I remembered about Mrs Shanahan. I quickly unpacked my clothes and brushed my hair. Mr Shanahan tapped at my bedroom door.

'Are you ready Krystyna?' he asked.

I opened the door and followed him down a short passageway. Mr Shanahan walked quickly and tapped on a door at the end of the passage. 'Marj,' he said, opening the door, 'I'd like you to meet Krystyna.'

She was lying in bed with a blue bed-jacket around her shoulders. 'Hello child,' she said softly. 'Welcome.' Then her shoulders started heaving and I saw that she was crying.

'Marj, dearie,' Mr Shanahan said, putting his arm underneath her and shifting her around more comfortably on the pillows. 'Please don't cry now. The child is here and you might upset her.'

Mrs Shanahan sniffed and dried her tears on the corner of her bed-jacket. There was a border of tiny pink flowers embroidered along the bottom and I knew that she must have been the person who chose the wallpaper for my room. 'Perhaps we'd better have that cuppa,' Mr Shanahan said, tenderly tucking his wife further into bed. 'Come along, Krystyna.' He took me by the arm and led me from the bedroom gently and quietly, as if we were leaving the presence of someone important.

It was easy to settle into the routine of life at Reservoir Cottage. I loved waking up every morning in my room, pulling back the pink curtains and watching the dappled sun shadows drifting across the wall. I looked forward to each day and soon got used to Nan's large funny face. We were both different in our own way, and Nan spoke so slowly that I didn't feel so awkward when my English sometimes came out the wrong way.

Under Mrs Shanahan's directions from the bedroom, we did the cooking, the cleaning, the washing and the ironing. I loved the rhythm of the housework and felt included as a member of the household. I knew where to hang the tea towels after drying the dishes and where to empty the teapot. Knowing these things gave me a sense of belonging which I hadn't felt for a long time.

On Friday nights Nan and I dragged the tin bath into

the kitchen, heated up the bath water, and took turns to wash, stripping off all our clothes in the warm kitchen and soaping each other's back and neck. At first I felt shy of helping Nan wash her back and I was embarrassed to take my turn in the bath after her. But Nan loved bath night and I soon overcame my diffidence and joined in her fun. We made foam bubbles and blew them around the kitchen, we took turns to pour waterfalls over each other's heads, and sometimes we floated flowers from the garden in the bath and sat among them. Nan and I became friends. We went for long walks together, hand in hand. She showed me all her secret places in the fields and I taught her to say '*dzien dobri*'. I stopped feeling worried and nervous in case I did something wrong, because at Reservoir Cottage it didn't matter. No one laughed or pointed me out. At night I would lie in my soft white bed with the summer breeze wafting in through the open window, dreaming that I had come home.

Even though she spent most her time in bed, Mrs Shanahan was at the centre of the household. I was drawn closer by her gentleness and it soon became my job to take in her morning cup of tea. At night I liked to kneel beside her bed and say my prayers and she would lie there with her hand resting gently on the top of my head. Sometimes she would talk for a while, telling me about the places where she had lived and the jobs she had done. Mr Shanahan had been a shepherd and she'd done the cooking on a lot of high-country places, preparing food for eight or ten men.

'But it's hard always moving on,' she said one night,

tapping me on the shoulder. 'Once we had Nan I just wanted to settle down.'

I nodded and smiled because it seemed to me that Mrs Shanahan's life was full of sadness. She was often unwell and sometimes I heard her crying out with pain in the night. Mr Shanahan told me that she had a cancer, but when I was with her we never talked about her illness. Sometimes we just sat together holding hands on top of the blankets and I thought about my own mother who had died in the filth on the floor. My heart ached to talk about her to Mrs Shanahan, because I knew that she would understand. But when I looked down at her lying there on the bed I could not speak because I knew that she too was dying and I didn't want to burden her. It seemed so sad to me that death had to come and take the people whom I loved.

After breakfast in the mornings I usually spent an hour chopping wood. Mr Shanahan gave me a hatchet of my own and showed me how to split the logs with clean sharp blows. I liked the heavy feel of the axe-head in my hand, but the sharp pungent smell of freshly cut pine reminded me of the camp in Siberia and the dreary cold days when my stomach churned and there was nothing to eat. I stacked the wood I cut in tidy piles under the lean-to beside the back door and thought how strange and distant the punishing labour in the Siberian forest seemed now. Life was so warm and comfortable here and there was a natural rhythm to the day that had been missing from my life for as long as I could remember. Each day's tasks had a measured orderliness that was in step with the change of the seasons and the day's weather. In the evenings Mr Shanahan would tap the barometer and tell us what the weather would be tomorrow. It was a comforting feeling to know that even when it rained and thundered there would be enough wood chopped outside the back door and we could take shelter together at Reservoir Cottage.

It seemed as if every day I learned something new. Mr Shanahan showed me how to sharpen an axe, how to tie knots and make a tinder fire. In the garden I learned from Nan how to separate the baby bulbs so that there would be more flowers in the spring, and in the evenings I sat beside Mrs Shanahan and learned how to crochet. I made a cushion cover out of red and white wool, and when I had finished sewing it together I piled it among the cushions on the settee. It stood out with its vivid colours and Mr Shanahan called it the Polish cushion, which made me laugh, but I knew that they would keep calling it that even when I had gone back to school and I felt glad that I would leave some trace of myself in this place.

This was something that troubled me: I needed to have concrete reminders of the places I had been because I seemed to be losing recollections of my Polish past. There were fragments that stuck in my mind like pictures, but my home, the barracks in Siberia and even the face of my sister were fading. Many of the things that I could remember made me cry, but crying felt like a sort of weakness so I tried not to think about things that were sad. When I closed my eyes at night I often saw the face of my dead mother as they shoved her out of the cattle truck on to the pile of corpses.

I tried to think about cheerful things and to chase my mother's image from my mind but it was all that I had left of her and I needed to remember what she looked like. Sometimes it tormented me and I would lie awake at night, weeping and wondering why my mother's face was still here to haunt me. I wanted to speak about it, but I was afraid. I didn't want to tell anyone about the dark shadows that lingered in my mind.

Mr Shanahan seemed almost to understand without my speaking. On the mornings when I got up with a dull headache and aching eyes, we would set off together on some outdoor chore that soon made my eyes sparkle. One morning as I sat quietly in the kitchen drinking tea and trying to throw off the burdens of the night he called me to the back door.

'Hey, Krystyna,' he shouted, 'have you seen this bobby dazzler?' I went to the back door and stared out. Mr Shanahan was holding a bike and grinning like mad. 'I've dug out Marj's old bike,' he said. 'We used to go off together when we were courting. D'you know how to ride?'

I blushed and shook my head.

'Well hop on and I'll give you a push.'

Nan stood in the doorway watching as I climbed on to the seat and reached for the pedals. She giggled and waved as I wavered from side to side trying to get my balance.

'I'll hang on for a bit,' Mr Shanahan said, right behind me. 'That way you'll be able to get the hang of it.' He pushed the bike down the garden path and out on to the road. I clung to the handlebars. 'Okay then, let's go ..' He started running along the road, giving the bike a hefty push. It was my job to steer. The pedals sprang around and around and I could only just keep my feet on. Steering was even harder and I grabbed the handlebars hard and stared down into the dusty shingle ruts. 'Right-ohhh …' Mr Shanahan was yelling, 'you're on your own!'

Suddenly my legs were pumping, the handlebars were woggling but I was biking along by myself. I pushed harder on the pedals and felt as if I was flying. The fields beside me passed as if in a blur. I took my eyes from the road for just a minute, glancing back to see if I could catch a glimpse of Mr Shanahan, and in that instant the handlebars started veering all over the place. The bike and I smacked to the ground.

I felt the gravel bite into my face, my legs and my hands. I tried to stand up, but my cardigan was twisted around the frame, and I lay there on the road, tangled up with Mr Shanahan's bike, shouting to myself in Polish. I was so angry because learning to ride a bike was really important to me. Among the girls at school there seemed to be some sort of shame at not knowing how to ride, and I wanted to be able to join their cycling excursions and picnics. There was a rolling cloud of dust along the road as Mr Shanahan came towards me in the Vauxhall.

'Good on you, kiddo,' he said jumping out of the car and heaving the bike upright. My cardigan twisted and tore along the seam.

'My cardigan!' I sobbed.

'Let's see now,' Mr Shanahan said, examining the tear. 'Well, it's not really my department. We'll have to get Marj to have a look at it. Now, how badly hurt are you?' He pulled me up on to my feet and inspected my bleeding legs, face and hands. 'Better get you back home,' he said, opening the car boot and putting the wheel of the bike in. 'We'll save the biking for tomorrow.'

I think I fell in love with Mr Shanahan. He was such fun to be with, and he was always patient and kind to Nan. He loved to make her laugh and they would sit together at the kitchen table making up poems and chuckling loudly. Nan didn't go to school but Mr Shanahan taught her to write, and in the evenings she would copy Tennyson's poems from a worn brown book, writing the same lines over and over until she had them right. Mrs Shanahan watched over the household like an ailing angel but she seemed to know when the blackcurrants were ripe and which hens had stopped laying. One evening when I was sitting in her room chatting, she suddenly sat straight up in bed.

'Is something the matter?' I asked, jumping to my feet.

'Yes,' she said, but her eyes were smiling. 'It's the Fairlie show this weekend and you've got to go.' She sent me looking for Mr Shanahan, and the two of them started to get really excited. They talked about merinos and wethers, two-tooths and weaners, and whether or not Mrs Maggs from down the road was busy. Someone had to be around to keep an eye on Mrs Shanahan as we would be away all day.

Reservoir Cottage was full of excitement. Nan went to bed early that night and in the morning she gurgled and chortled so much to herself that she couldn't eat more than a mouthful of toast. Straight after breakfast Mrs Shanahan called me into her room.

'Have a look in the wardrobe, Krystyna,' she said. 'There might be something in there that you'd like to wear.' I felt myself blushing because I knew that she must have noticed that my summer dress was too small for me. 'Go on, dear,' Mrs Shanahan urged. 'They're old things that I've been saving for years but Nan will never fit any of them and I reckon I was once your size.' I opened the door of the old oak wardrobe. Inside there was a row of dresses hanging in front of a rather heavy-looking suit. 'Oh, I used to be a fancy dresser,' Mrs Shanahan said as I carefully fingered the dresses. 'My Mum was a dab hand with the sewing machine and she'd whip me up a new skirt in one afternoon.'

I wanted to ask her about falling in love with Mr Shanahan but I was too shy. Instead we talked about styles and fabrics, dresses and patterns. I tried on some of her dresses and stood in the window where she could easily see me from her bed. We laughed at the ones that didn't fit and bunched up in all the wrong places. By the end of the afternoon I had a stack of five or six dresses that Mrs Shanahan had decided to give me.

'You'd better leave most of them here and I'll send them on to you at school,' Mrs Shanahan said, 'otherwise the nuns might think you've got a secret admirer.'

Mrs Shanahan seemed to care about me in a way that no one else did. Sometimes I wanted to throw myself on her bed and feel her arms around me, telling me that everything would be all right and that I would be able to stay at Reservoir Cottage forever. Instead I had to steel myself for the day when the summer holidays ended and I would have to leave Mrs Shanahan and go back to school. I envied Nan being Mrs Shanahan's daughter. I wished that she could be my mother too.

On Show Day I got up and washed myself carefully before putting on Marjorie Shanahan's crepe de chine dress. It was a soft pale pink with little covered buttons all the way up the bodice, and underneath I wore a borrowed corset which nearly fitted and smelt a bit musty. Shoes were a problem because all Mrs Shanahan's dainty pairs were too small for me, so I wore my black school shoes with their heavy tread.

'Whoo … ee!' Mr Shanahan whistled when I came out into the kitchen. 'You look great, Krystyna.' Nan tapped her father on the shoulder and twirled around to show off her best dress. 'You too, Nan,' he said, giving her a kiss on the forehead. 'And now, ladies, let's go to the show.'

The Fairlie Agricultural and Pastoral Show was held in the showgrounds on the outskirts of the town. We parked the car in a grassy paddock and headed straight for the pigs.

'They've got the biggest and the best,' Mr Shanahan told us, leading the way past rows and rows of pens in which pigs wallowed in huge piles of dirty straw. The smell was sweet and steamy.

'Pooh!' Nan said. 'It stinks.'

We went on to see enormous bulls straining at the sides of their pens, and gentle cows with great big soft velvet faces and huge dribbling lips that smelt of warm grass. We looked at hundreds of sheep with banks of wool growing on their backs and they stared back at us with spooky scared eyes, bleating softly. Everywhere we went there were men tickling and scratching the animals in the pens. Some were standing by in white coats ready to collect wheelbarrows full of steaming dung as soon as it fell from the animal's bottom. Nan and I held hands and stared around the shed. The smell reminded me of our stables at home in Poland where Tata had kept the farm horses. Mr Shanahan was right at home. He patted cows, peered at sheep's teeth and pulled a strand or two of wool right off a sheep's back. Nan was restless and after a while she started tugging at her father's arm.

'I want to go to the baking,' she said, repeating her sentence two or three times to get Mr Shanahan's attention.

'Off you go then,' Mr Shanahan said, hardly able to take his eyes off a horned merino ram. 'Don't lose each other and I'll see you in the afternoon tea tent about three.'

I followed Nan into a huge shed which was crowded with women peering into glass cases. 'Cakes,' Nan announced, pushing her way through the queue. For the next two hours we gazed at a wondrous display of housewifely talents. There were rows of lamingtons and sponges, fruit cakes and chocolate cakes, iced and plain. There were piles of pikelets, scones and gems, bath buns, rock cakes and queenies … I felt dizzy. There was nothing that resembled the cakes my mother and her Polish friends used to make. I could still remember the taste of Mama's *makowiec*, sweet and golden with a sticky layer of poppy seeds all the way through. Standing among the crowds of women staring at the baking, I was suddenly overwhelmed with longing for Poland, for the warmth of my home kitchen and the sight of my mother standing there. I wanted to be among things and people who were familiar to me. I wanted to grow up to be a woman in my own homeland. I felt dazed by the crowds of women pressing around me and wanted to find somewhere quiet to sit down, but Nan was beside me tapping my arm and she led me past glass cases filled with jars of jam. There was raspberry and blackberry, plum and apricot, grapefruit and carrot marmalades, apple jellies flavoured with mint and cloves. The jars glistened with the evidence of hours of dedicated preparation, but their merits blurred in front of my eyes. All around the shed there were groups of women standing talking together. They seemed to know each other and many of them said 'Hello' to Nan and stared curiously at me. I felt like an imposter. I had never made jam, except in Siberia where Mama boiled the wild berries without sugar, but I knew that these things were secrets that I should keep to myself. All around me women were swapping recipes and hints about cooking and I had to pinch my arm to restrain myself from running back to the baking display and grabbing some food. I couldn't just look at all this food and admire it. I still needed to eat, to stuff food into my mouth to bury the memories of those terrible times when there wasn't anything at all to eat. I pushed my way past the women and outside into the fresh air. Nan came hurrying behind me.

'I'm so hungry,' she said.

I told her that I was hungry too and we struggled through the crowds to find the refreshment tent. It was packed with people eating and drinking and we passed from group to group, trying to catch sight of Nan's dad. There was no sign of him. A man bought me an orangeade which I shared with Nan, and she grabbed a couple of scones left behind on a table. We sat on a bench and ate them, keeping our eyes on the door, but I didn't recognise Mr Shanahan when he finally turned up. His eyes were bloodshot and he couldn't walk straight. He staggered into the refreshment tent and walked straight into a tent pole.

'Here, watch where you're going, sonny,' he said, and gave the pole a thwack. The waitresses laughed. 'Where are you, girls?' he called loudly.

'Over here!' I grabbed Nan's hand and pulled her up with me.

'I want to go home now, Dada,' Nan whimpered, tugging at his arm.

'Non ... sense, girlie,' Mr Shanahan said in a slow, slurry sort of way. 'Tonight's the night for dancing.'

Even though he was drunk Mr Shanahan still had an easygoing air about him. We bought fish and chips and sat under the mainstreet trees to eat them. Nan was tired and kept saying that she wanted to go home. Mr Shanahan bought her a huge hokey-pokey ice cream to console her. When she finished we walked back to the car and Nan climbed into the back and fell asleep.

'It's just you and me now, kiddo,' Mr Shanahan said,

winking. 'On with the dancing.'

I wasn't sure that I liked Mr Shanahan in his happy drunk mood and I didn't know what he meant by dancing. At Pahiatua Camp we had a dancing group which practised every day and gracefully performed traditional Polish dances for the rest of us. I had not been to any New Zealand dancing and wished that I could ask Mr Shanahan about what would happen, but he was tapping the steering wheel and singing away to himself so I kept quiet. We drove through Fairlie to the Oddfellows Hall. It was nearing dark now, but the whole place was alive with car lights. Women were climbing out of cars and straightening their dresses while the men seemed to be clustered together drinking out of brown paper bags. Mr Shanahan parked well away from the noise around the hall and carefully covered Nan with a blanket.

'She'll be all right,' he said. 'I'll look in on her every hour or so. Now let's go.'

I straightened my dress, smoothed my hair and followed him towards the hall. Mr Shanahan stumbled and swore as we walked across the uneven carpark. 'Block your ears, m'dear,' he said, but I listened anyway because I was interested in learning new words. That night I learned bloody, bugger, shit and damn.

Mr Shanahan paid at the doorway and we walked into the brightly lit hall. In a couple of seconds Mr Shanahan had disappeared among a huge clump of men standing around the door. They were all talking and smoking, clapping each other on the back and telling jokes. Along the sides of the hall the women were sitting on benches, talking and laughing together. I was uncertain about what to do, and backed into the corner by the door, hoping that no one would notice me. I felt very lonely because the only person I knew was Mr Shanahan. The noise of people talking seemed like a wall around me, and I was glad when the music started. The band began with a foxtrot and the men stopped lounging around the doorway and surged towards the women, offering an arm to the one whom they'd chosen as their partner. I stood in my corner watching, hoping that no one would offer me their arm because I had no idea how to do the complicated steps that the others seemed to know so well. But even though I couldn't dance I loved the music. It swayed through my body so that I was dancing in spite of myself, shifting from leg to leg in my corner as the partners in front of me circled around the room.

It was a long lonely evening as the band played dance after dance. I watched the partners moving together, holding their bodies and staring into each other's eyes. I wondered what it would be like being so close to a man, feeling his breath on your face and his arms around you. Then the band played a quick-moving bracket and announced that it was supper time. Couples grabbed each other by the hand and raced towards the supper room. I shyly joined the other unescorted ladies and filed into a room that seemed full of people and trestle tables laden with food. I was handed a plate, but for the first time I could remember I didn't feel hungry. The food seemed to be part of the intimacy of the dancing. Men were offering their wives and girlfriends plates of bacon pinwheels and scones with cream and jam. Women were smiling up into the eyes of their men friends and husbands, offering another cup of tea and pretending to ignore the smell of beer on the men's breaths. I felt that I was present at some sort of ritual of man and woman love that I didn't understand, and went outside to wait in the car with Nan. It took a while to find. All over the car park there were couples leaning against the vehicles, kissing passionately. I didn't know anything about kissing. It seemed like a strange thing to be doing outside in the dark when you could be inside eating.

My holiday at Reservoir Cottage suddenly came to an end. Summer seemed to pass so quickly, and too soon it was time to return to school.

'You're a lovely girl, Krystyna,' Mrs Shanahan said when I went to kiss her goodbye. 'Now hold up your head and be proud of being Polish.'

But at school it was like sinking under the current again. The girls in my dormitory talked about nothing but boyfriends and dances. I was left out of these long discussions because someone had seen me at the dance in Fairlie and word had got around that I'd sat in the corner all evening.

I tried to concentrate on my schoolwork. I wanted to do well in the coming exams in order to prove to my teachers and classmates that I wasn't stupid. I needed to be able to be good at something, and studying gave me a sense of satisfaction as well as an excuse to ignore the other girls.

Then my period came, a rusty reddish-brown bloodstain

in my knickers. I thought I must be dying and hid them in the bottom of my drawer, forgetting about the nuns' inspections, and waited to see what my body would do next. We were standing in a dormitory line the next morning when Sister Immaculata pulled my knickers out of a bag.

'A dirty filthy girl left these in her drawer,' she said severely. 'She knows who she is and I want her to remain behind. Class dismissed.'

Everyone left the dormitory except me. Sister Immaculata stood staring at me, her face twisted with disgust.

'Jesus, Mary and Joseph,' she said. 'Never in my twenty-five years in this convent have I seen anything so disgusting.' I stood with my eyes on the floor, biting my lips, digging my fingernails into my hands. 'Such filth!' The Sister was angry. 'But what can we expect from you Polish girls?' she shouted. I tried hard not to cry. I stood there like stone, blocking my ears to whatever she was saying. I felt so dirty and ashamed but I could also feel the blood starting to trickle down my leg. I clenched my thighs together and willed it to stop.

'You're going straight to the Reverend Mother,' Sister Immaculata said, grabbing me by the ear. It hurt but I kept quiet, walking sideways beside her along the corridor. She pushed me through the office door and stood behind me with her arms folded.

'Thank you, Sister,' Reverend Mother said, 'you may leave us together.'

The Reverend Mother always made me feel nervous, but as the door shut behind me I felt relief.

'Sit down, Christine,' she said, pointing to the chair in front of her desk. She was kindly but distant and she seemed to be looking at me from a long way off. 'Now tell me what has happened.' I stuttered and stumbled through the story about the bloodstained knickers, feeling hot with embarrassment. I didn't know if it was all right to talk to the Reverend Mother about it, but I needed to know about the blood I could still feel trickling from my body. I needed to know whether I was going to live or die.

Reverend Mother sat watching me. There was a few moments' silence after I'd finished talking. I felt so confused. Part of me wanted to hide from her steady stare and the other part of me wanted to throw myself against her body to try to force some comfort from her. Instead she said a Hail Mary and told me that it was normal for a girl to bleed from her body. She unlocked a cupboard behind her desk and gave me a pile of white towels to soak up the blood. 'Wash these in the laundry before morning prayers,' she said. 'Now go back to your classroom.'

I left the Reverend Mother's office with the towels under my arm and went to the toilets to cry. I felt as lonely as I had when my mother died. I had needed her then and I needed her now.

I plunged myself into my studies and that year I passed my School Certificate examinations. Some of my classmates started leaving school and Miss Hight, the commercial practice teacher, asked me where I had set my sights.

'I'm sorry,' I told her, 'I don't know what you mean.'

210

'What are you going to do with your life, Christine?' she asked. 'You'll be fifteen soon and it's time you started earning a living.'

I'd never thought about leaving school and having a job, and I had no idea how I might go about making a life of my own. The idea appalled me.

Miss Hight must have sensed my hesitation, because she started bringing me copies of the Timaru Herald. 'Have a look through Situations Vacant,' she said every day. 'There might be something there for you.'

I didn't know what I was looking for. The jobs said things like office junior, secretary and bank clerk. How could I manage those? At school everyone knew that I was Polish, and although it did not make me popular, at least I could ask about words and phrases I still didn't know. And where would I live? I had never lived outside an institution; Danuta, Eva and Zofia had already left for the North Island. I was on my own.

I lay awake at nights worrying about what would happen to me and where I would go. I went to see the Reverend Mother and asked her if I could stay in the convent.

'My dear,' she said, 'you can only stay here if you have a vocation.' She folded her hands one on top of the other.

'But Reverend Mother,' I whispered, sitting on the edge of my chair, 'I have nowhere else to go.'

'We will help you, my child,' she said.

I sighed and left her office.

With Miss Hight's help I applied for and got a job in

the ticket office at the Timaru Railway Station. I packed my LMC case, said goodbye to the remainder of my classmates and went boarding at the home of an elderly widow whom the Reverend Mother knew. I envied the girls who were still at school. They seemed so sure of themselves and where they were going. Some wanted to go nursing and others were applying for entry to teachers' college. I felt cut off from these options.

I went to work at eight o' clock in the morning wearing a dress that Reverend Mother had given me. It was too long but I bunched it up around my waist and wore my school cardigan over the top. All I had to do was take the money and stamp the tickets, answer the phone and make the bookings. People were always °asking if I was 'the Polish girl' and I'd get hot and embarrassed because I was trying hard to be like them and not to stand out. I didn't want to be Polish any more.

I had morning and afternoon tea with Mr Cross, the station master, who brought a supply of food in cake tins that he kept on a shelf in the booking office. On my second day he offered me a piece of cake. I shook my head, unsure of whether to take it. 'Go on,' he said, 'Mum made it.'

So I took the cake and ate it up, savouring the sweet mouthfuls. I wondered how old Mr Cross's mother was but decided not to ask him and pretended that I didn't speak very much English. I felt unsure of myself in this new situation and was watchful, always careful not to do the wrong thing, not to say mixed-up words or speak out of turn. I knew that this job had been given to me as a favour and I tried to be good at it. I arranged the coins in tidy piles and answered the telephone politely. I smiled at the people who stood at the window to buy tickets and gave them the correct change. But I shuddered each time a train drew in at the station, and the piercing whistle made me sweat with fear. Sometimes I had to crouch behind the desk and hold my hands over my ears as the trains thundered through on the main trunk line. By the end of the day my head ached and my hands shook. I walked as fast as I could away from the railway station and the sound of the wheels on the tracks.

Mrs Ryan, the widow, lived in a house overlooking Caroline Bay and you couldn't see or hear the railway track. I had my own room at the back of the house with one heavily curtained window, but it was space to myself where I could cry without anyone watching me. At night I suffered from nightmares. The noise of the trains ran through my head. The hooting, the hissing and the shunting that I heard all day tormented me as soon as I closed my eyes. I lay rigid with fear as I saw my mother, my sister and my brother crowding into that cattle truck which took them away to die. In the morning I got up in the deathly silence of the widow's house and walked to the railway station where I worked.

Every week I got paid. I'd never had any money of my own before and now I held out my hand and received ten shillings. 'You're a good girl, Christine,' Mr Cross said as I signed the wages book. I tucked the money into my pocket, hardly able to wait for the day to end. After work I went shopping downtown, buying myself a slab of chocolate, a pair of stockings and a world map. I spent ages in the shops looking at things I wanted, and could have simply by handing over the money. I looked at shoes, hats, handbags and dresses. All my life I had worn things that had been handed down to me. The colour, size and style had meant nothing, and I'd been grateful just to have something to wear. Now I wanted to decide for myself some of the things that had always been chosen for me. I lingered in the shops, longing to have enough money to buy dresses in glowing colours and a hat with a ribbon around it.

I took the world map back to Mrs Ryan's and pinned it on the wall of my bedroom, marking the places I could remember going to with a piece of string. When she came to call me for dinner Mrs Ryan asked me to take the map down.

'The pins mark the wall,' she said, and then she took the opportunity to tell me once again about the death of her husband and how she came in from the garden and found him lying on the floor. 'It was a massive stroke,' she said, nodding her head wisely. 'All over in ten seconds. There was nothing anyone could have done for him, nothing at all.' She still had his suits hanging in the wardrobe and his hat was on the stand in the hall. 'They're too good to give to the Sally Army,' she was always saying. 'Feel the cloth … it'll last for ever.'

I soon became accustomed to her routine. Every morning she went to Mass to pray for her dead husband. In the evenings she recited the prayers for the dead while I knelt beside her, joining in the refrain 'May the eternal light shine upon him.' On my first evening I cried and Mrs Ryan made me cocoa. She thought it was lovely that I was so sad about her husband, but it was my mother I was crying for. My mother and all those thousands of dead bodies that I had seen piled high in the middle of nowhere. *Niech odpoczywaja na wieki*. May they rest forever.

I realised that I would have to get used to being misunderstood, to being called Christine instead of Krystyna. But I needed to understand the past which had brought me here to New Zealand. I joined the Public Library and spent my lunch time reading, trying to find out what had happened to the thousands of Poles deported like me. I scanned the books, looking for facts that connected my past and my present. I longed to stop being haunted by the shadows and the deaths of the past. But more than anything else I wanted to know why it had happened to me. I read everything I could find about the Second World War, about the invasions of Poland by Hitler, about the concentration camps and the massacre of the Jews, but there was no mention anywhere of our deportation or of the labour camps in Siberia.

At the railway station I tried to steel myself against the noise of the trains and to put milk in first when I poured the tea. I let the station master put his arm around me and call me dearie even though I didn't like the closeness and the smell of alcohol on his breath. At dinner time I ate shepherd's pie and boiled cabbage with Mrs Ryan and listened to her chatter about Mr Ryan and the weather. I felt lonely and longed for something in my life that reflected the richness of my Polish past. I covered my loneliness with reading. I spent hours looking at the map which I kept folded under my pillow, trying to make sense of the journey that had brought me here.

One day when I came home from work, Mrs Ryan was standing in the hall with a letter. 'It's for you,' she said. She stood beside me while I read my name on the front of the envelope. 'Who would be writing to you, then?' she asked.

'I don't know,' I told her, and ran quickly upstairs to my room to open it. My letter was from Madame Swietlicka who had been in charge of the Pahiatua Camp. In beautiful flowing Polish she was writing to tell me that a hostel for Polish working girls had been opened at Lyall Bay in Wellington. The Reverend Mother had written to tell her that I had left school, and they were holding me a place at the hostel if I wanted to come and work in Wellington. I read the letter over and over, laughing and crying as the things that were familiar to me came crowding in. I would be amongst Poles again! We had all lost our country, our homes and our families, but between us there was a closeness that bound us together. I ran downstairs to tell Mrs Ryan.

'Very nice, Christine,' she said, ladling out dollops of mashed potato. 'Don't forget that we agreed on three weeks' notice. Now I'll have to find someone else to take the room.'

I nodded and sat down to dinner. Even a repeat of the story of Mr Ryan's death did not dim my happiness. I slept soundly that night and in the morning I went to work half an hour early so I could tell Mr Cross my news. He wasn't pleased.

'You mean you're leaving, Christine?' he asked. I nodded happily. 'But … I gave you this job as a special favour. There was no question of you leaving. I need someone here for a long time.'

I said I was sorry and showed him the letter from Wellington. Mr Cross read it and frowned.

'If you ask me, young lady, you're taking a backward step,' he said sternly. 'You people need to get out and learn how we do things in this country. The sooner you forget about Poland and get on with being a Kiwi the better.'

I sighed and made a pot of tea. I didn't expect Mr Cross to understand the leap of joy inside me at the thought of being able to speak Polish again. I couldn't tell him of the burden of memories that lay heavy on my heart and how the noise of the trains tormented me. All day I answered the phone, sold tickets and chatted to my customers in English, knowing that soon I would be able to speak again in the language that was my own.

My last week at the railway station went quickly. The news soon got around the regular customers that I was leaving, and many of them stopped at the ticket office to say goodbye. Some of them brought me presents. Bunches of dahlias and sweetly scented stocks, cakes for morning tea, and one woman gave me several pots of blackcurrant jam. 'It'll build you up in the winter,' she said, shoving the parcel through the gap in the ticket window. 'And good luck to you, Christine.'

Mr Cross and I ate our way through most of the cakes and I took the leftovers home to Mrs Ryan.

'Oh,' she said, 'you must have made a bit of a hit. What's in the other parcel?' I showed her the jam. Mrs Ryan looked delighted. 'Blackcurrant's my favourite.' So I gave the pots to her because the sight of the dark fruity jam made me remember my mother licking the boiled fruit paste off pieces of bark in Siberia. I wished that she could have lived long enough to come to this country where food was so abundant.

On my last day at the ticket office Mr Cross announced that he was taking me out to lunch.

'But I have my lunch here,' I said, showing him the mutton and pickle sandwiches that Mrs Ryan made for me every day. 'Come along, my dear,' he said, taking me by the arm. 'This is my treat.'

So I closed the ticket office and we walked down the road to the Railway Hotel where we sat opposite one another in the dark dining room. Mr Cross ordered roast beef and yorkshire pudding for both of us.

'And what will you have to drink?' he asked, taking hold of my hand as I fiddled with my fork.

'A glass of water, please,' I said, taking my hand away. I felt hemmed in, sitting there in the stuffy dining room with its heavy curtains on either side of the narrow windows. I wanted to run outside and feel the air on my face and pay a last visit to the Public Library.

'Come on, my dear,' Mr Cross said. 'This is the last time I'll see you for a while. Let's have a little sherry.' He ordered a whisky for himself and a sherry for me which came in a tiny glass with gold around the rim.

'Thank you,' I said, raising the glass and sipping. It was a strong sweet taste that made my stomach glow.

'That's better,' Mr Cross said, swallowing his whisky. 'Now you will be nice to me today, won't you Chrissie?'

I let him hold my hand again, even though I wanted to pull away from his grasping fingers. Our meals arrived on thick white plates and he had to let go of my hand to eat, but his legs kept rubbing up against mine underneath the table. The thick slices of beef smothered in gravy sickened me.

'Come on now, dearie ... eat up,' Mr Cross kept saying, and he ordered another whisky and a sherry. I drank down the brown liquid and it made my head swim. The meat was tough, sinewy and hard to swallow. Mr Cross ate forkful after forkful of meat, gravy, peas, carrots and potato all loaded methodically onto his fork so that there was a mixture of everything in each swallow. 'Now what about pudding?' he asked once he had eaten all the food on his plate.

I shook my head.

'Not hungry, eh?' Mr Cross said, calling for another whisky and leaning towards me across the table. 'So that's how you keep your pretty figure?' I sat in my chair not knowing where to look or what to do. I wanted to get away from this lunch for two and I felt silly sitting at this table with Mr Cross. It seemed as if he knew something that I didn't, and the way he kept reaching for my hand and nudging me with his knees made me feel uneasy. I felt a bit dizzy from the sherry and I looked around to see if I could find the Ladies.

'In the lobby on the right,' said the woman who was bringing Mr Cross a plate of steamed pudding and another drink. I got up from the table and left the dining room, stumbling against a table on my way out. 'Poor kid,' I heard her say to Mr Cross. 'Now you behave yourself, Jim.' And they both laughed.

I sat in the toilet and held my head in my hands, grateful that it was a little room on its own so that no one could see me. I felt sick and tried splashing my face with cold water to make myself feel better. There was a mirror over the basin and I stared at myself, seeing blue eyes, blonde hair and a forehead that I remembered on my mother. I saw nothing that was particularly Polish or that revealed how I felt inside. I felt a rush of nausea and ran to the toilet. The door of the Ladies opened and when I finished vomiting the woman who had waited on the table was standing there with a towel.

'Come along, lovie,' she said. 'Clean yourself up. His Lordship has finished his pud and gone back to the station.' She ran a basin of warm water and waited while I washed my face and hands. 'You're a pretty kid,' she said, leaning back against the wall and lighting a cigarette. 'But you look after yourself. Don't go letting old men get up to any funny business.'

I felt better now and thanked the woman.

'It's nothing,' she said. 'I read about all you kids in the

paper. My Mum died when I was eleven but I never had to go through anything like that.' She gave me a kiss on the cheek and pushed me out the door. 'Now get back to work and keep your wits about you,' she said, disappearing into the gloomy dining room.

I walked up the road back to the railway station. The last afternoon passed quickly. Mr Cross spent most of his time snoozing on a platform bench underneath his newspaper. I sold tickets and answered the telephone and at five o' clock Mr Cross gave me my pay.

'Got time for a quick drink?' he asked wistfully.

'I'm sorry,' I told him. 'I have to pack.'

The next day it was my turn to climb on a train at the Timaru station and travel north. I had a soft leather window seat and sat back watching the countryside pass in a blur of fields and fences, cows and sheep. I thought back to my first New Zealand train ride to Pahiatua Camp. Now I was used to the sight of hundreds of sheep and had even stayed in some of the small houses dotted across the landscape. I sat in the train listening to the familiar noise of the wheels on the track, a noise that seemed to have been with me all my life. So many times a train had taken me away from people and places that I loved and now it was taking me back to my own people.

Arriving at the Polish hostel in Lyall Bay was like coming home. I walked through the front door of a beautiful house with a huge cascading staircase, balconies, vast living rooms and a gracious garden. The whole building resounded with the noise of Polish being spoken. Girls whom I remembered from Persia and the Soviet Union threw their arms around me, kissing and crying, talking and laughing. Even the Ursuline nuns who ran the hostel spoke in Polish as they took me upstairs to show me my room, which I was to share with three other girls. I no longer wanted a room of my own. I had slept too long in the loneliness of Mrs Ryan's bedroom and now I revelled in the companionship of other girls. On the stairs, in the corridors and sitting in the huge dining room I saw faces that I could remember. My loneliness faded as girls reached out to touch me, to welcome me into their group. They were talking about their jobs, their clothes and their boyfriends, but even though I had to find a new job and I didn't have a boyfriend, it didn't seem to matter. Here was a place where I belonged, with people who had become my family in New Zealand.

Years later there was another family. The children whom I bore and the man I took to be my life's partner. He did not know about me and the place where I came from, but he loved my name and the fierceness of passion that brought us together. I learnt to do things the way New Zealand women did them and forgot how to cook pierogi and barscz. But I always remembered my home in Baranowiczie, so far away from the islands of New Zealand. Sometimes in the afternoon when the house was tidy and the children were at school I would sit in the sun remembering. It brought me no sadness now but I kept those things folded in a part of my mind where no one could reach them. The terror, the deportations, the hunger, the filth, the screams of the dying, how could I expect my children to understand such things? They had been born in a country of peace and plenty where mist wreaths the hills and the waves run blue-green in the sea.

There was a day when my daughter came asking. I had named her for my mother, even though she had brown hair and green eyes. She was a lovely child and we were happy together, as we shared a world that I was coming to know. As she grew up she looked at me with knowing, as if she saw into the shadows deep within my mind. She asked about my mother, about the place and country where I was born. There were so many things that she wanted to know.

I could only answer her with gaps and silence. I am old now and nearly past living, there are so many things I cannot recall. But for my daughter I reached back into the depth of the darkness and told her my story. She sat beside me crying, weeping the tears that I have not cried for a long time. She put *her arms around me, calling me Mama Kochana, and I sat beside her, silent and empty. My mother ... my brother ... my sister ... where are you now?*